T0387246

SELENA GOMEZ
Pop Singer and Actress

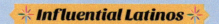

Influential Latinos

SELENA GOMEZ

Pop Singer and Actress

Enslow Publishing
101 W. 23rd Street
Suite 240
New York, NY 10011
USA

enslow.com

Jennifer Torres

Published in 2016 by Enslow Publishing, LLC
101 W. 23rd Street, Suite 240, New York, NY 10011

Copyright © 2016 by Enslow Publishing, LLC

All rights reserved.

No part of this book may be reproduced by any means without the written permission of the publisher.

Library of Congress Cataloging-in-Publication Data
Torres, Jennifer.
 Selena Gomez : pop singer and actress / Jennifer Torres.
   pages cm. — (Influential Latinos)
 Summary: "Describes the life of pop star Selena Gomez"— Provided by publisher.
 Includes bibliographical references and index.
 ISBN 978-0-7660-6999-2
 1. Gomez, Selena, 1992—Juvenile literature. 2. Actors—United States—Biography—Juvenile literature. 3. Singers—United States—Biography—Juvenile literature. I. Title.
 PN2287.G585T68 2015
 791.4302'8092—dc23
 [B]

                    2015015759

Printed in the United States of America

To Our Readers: We have done our best to make sure all Web site addresses in this book were active and appropriate when we went to press. However, the author and the publisher have no control over and assume no liability for the material available on those Web sites or on any Web sites they may link to. Any comments or suggestions can be sent by e-mail to customerservice@enslow.com.

Photo Credits: AF archive/Alamy, p. 50; Arlene Richie/Media Sources/Media Sources/The LIFE Images Collection/Getty Images, p. 19; Blend Images/Shutterstock.com, p. 25; Brian Babineau/WireImage/Getty Images, p. 106; Brian To/FilmMagic/Getty Images, p. 94; Chris Polk/KCA2010/Getty Images for KCA, p. 80; courtesy of the Everett Collection, pp. 36, 41, 59, 61, 69, 73, 83; D Free/Shutterstock.com, p. 43; gguy/Shutterstock.com, p. 16; Helga Esteb/Shutterstock.com, p. 110; James Devaney/WireImage/Getty Images, p. 77; Jean-Paul Aussenard/WireImage/Getty Images, p. 20; Jeff Kravitz/AMA2011/FilmMagic/Getty Images, p. 72; Jeff Kravitz/AMA2014/FilmMagic/Getty Images, p. 88; John Shearer/WireImage/Getty Images, p. 96; Jn Kopaloff/FilmMagic/Getty IMages, p. 6; Kevin Mazur/Fox/WireImage/Getty Images, p. 11; Kevin Mazur/TCA 2012/WireImage/Getty Images, p. 102; K Mazur/TCA 2008/WireImage/Getty Images, pp. 45, 48, 71; Kevin Winter/Getty Images Entertainment/Getty Images, p. 8. 65; Kevin Winter/NBC Universal/Getty Images, p. 85; Mark Sullivan/WireImage/Getty Images, p. 90; patrice6000/Shutterstock.com, p. 30; s_buckley/Shutterstock.com, pp. 3, 23, 29, 31, 33, 104; San Antonio Express-News/ZUMA Press, p. 53; Stefania D'Alessandro/Getty Images Entertainment/Getty images, p. 87; Theo Wargo/WireImage for Glamour Magazine/Getty Images, p. 98.

Cover Credit: s_bukley/Shutterstock.com (Selena Gomez at 2013 Teen Choice Awards).

Contents

1. A Night to Remember........ 7
2. Just a Small Town Girl...... 17
3. Endings and New Beginnings.................... 27
4. A Natural Talent............. 37
5. Leaving *Barney* Behind..... 47
6. Disney Dreams................ 57
7. There's a New Wizard in Town...................... 67
8. And Then There Was Justin 79
9. More to Life than Fame and Fortune.................. 91
10. Over the Rainbow.......... 101

Chronology................... 112

Chapter Notes............... 115

Glossary 121

Further Reading 123

Index......................... 125

Actress and singer Selena Gomez has been in the entertainment industry for most of her young life.

Chapter 1

A Night to Remember

When Selena Gomez ascended the stage of the Shrine Auditorium in Los Angeles, a thunderous roar of applause echoed from a sparkling audience of celebrities that included Taylor Swift, Jennifer Lopez, Demi Lovato, and Ariana Grande. Wearing a sleek black pantsuit, her hair pulled neatly back into a low ponytail, Selena made her way to the podium during the 2014 Teen Choice Awards on August 10, 2014. The show's hosts, *Modern Family*'s Sarah Hyland and *Teen Wolf*'s Tyler Posey, presented her with the most prestigious award of the night: The Ultimate Choice Award.

The award—which comes in the form of a custom-designed surfboard to signify the freedom teenagers have in the summer—has been referred to as this generation's version of a lifetime achievement award. That night, it was awarded in recognition of Selena's "extraordinary contributions to the entertainment world."[1]

SELENA GOMEZ: POP SINGER AND ACTRESS

Gomez accepted the Ultimate Choice Award—a surfboard—at the 2014 Teen Choice Awards.

A Night to Remember

The video montage of Selena's work on television, in movies, and in music, was extensive for a young woman of twenty-two. As her many accomplishments were splashed across the monitors, Selena knew she wasn't the only one who deserved accolades. Tonight it wasn't her contributions Selena wanted to acknowledge—it was her mothers'. "I want to thank my mom so much because she's the greatest human being in the world and she's strong and she's given up her life for me and she's so beautiful," Gomez said. "I want all of you to love your mom and give her everything because she's incredible."[1] Then, pointing to the surfboard, she added, "This is for you. This never belongs to me. This is for you."[2]

That night Selena joined the ranks of past winners that have included Ashton Kutcher, Kristen Stewart, Justin Timberlake, and Britney Spears. At twenty-two, she was the youngest to ever receive the honor.

In addition to her mother, she wanted to thank her fans. "I have to be honest, especially this month, I cannot thank you guys enough. You remind me amidst all the stuff that we deal with personally, you remind me of what's important. That's giving and loving and caring about each other," Selena said. "I'm not trying to preach, but you guys make me better."[3]

Perhaps she was referring to a tumultuous year of both professional highs as well as some very personal lows centering around on her on again-off again relationship with fellow pop star, Justin Bieber.

Rough Start

The year had started on a sour note when on January 5, 2014 Selena checked into The Meadows, a psychiatric facility for the treatment of trauma and addiction in Arizona. Her representative at the time said it was a voluntary stay that did not involve any substance abuse issues.

In a statement to her fans Selena addressed the issue personally. "My fans are so important to me and I would never want to disappoint them. But it has become clear to me and those close to me that after many years of putting my work first, I need to spend some time on myself in order to be the best person I can be. To my fans, I sincerely apologize and I hope you guys know how much each and every one of you means to me."[4]

After canceling over a dozen tour dates, she was back to work on March 29, just in time to attend the 2014 Kids Choice Awards held at the University of Southern California Galen Center in Los Angeles. Selena was lucky enough not to get "slimed" and even luckier to win the award for Favorite Female Singer, triumphing over Lady Gaga, Katy Perry, and her good friend Taylor Swift.

Selena was also presented with the coveted Fan Army Award, which was a direct result of her massive fan base—known as The Selenators. The competition pinned her fans against other celebrity fan groups: The Arianators (Ariana Grande), The Directioners (One Direction), and the JT Superfans (Justin Timberlake).

A Night to Remember

Modern Family's Sarah Hyland hosted the Teen Choice Awards and presented Gomez with her Ultimate Award.

Fans had to compete in daily trials on social media to win, and Selena's fans came out on top.

Speaking to her fans as she accepted her award, Selena recognized their continued support. "I just have to say that you guys have been the most loyal, dedicated people in my life," she said, "because you continuously, every year, bless me with the opportunity to do what I love, so thank you so much." "You guys are awesome, and this is for you. So, thank you."[5]

The evening also created a stir on social media, when Selena was spotted wearing a gold band on her left hand. Speculation was rampant that Justin Bieber has proposed. But in truth, things with Justin were not going well. Rumors of Bieber's infidelity swirled as photos emerged of him spending time with other women in Canada that week. Just a few days prior to the Kids Choice Awards, Selena was approached by a person who handed her a subpoena to testify in a lawsuit against Bieber by a paparazzi who claimed he was "physically attacked" by the superstar in May 2012 while trying to photograph Bieber and Gomez at a California shopping center.

Despite the difficult moments, it was a year of great accomplishment for the Latina star. In addition to three major awards from Teen Choice and Kids Choice, Selena also won honors for her song "Come & Get It" at both the Broadcast Music, Inc. (BMI) Pop Awards and the American Society of Composers, Authors and Publishers (ASCAP) Pop Music Awards.

A Night to Remember

Getting Slimed

Other than the coveted orange blimp given out as the award, The Nickelodeon Kids' Choice Awards are best known for one thing—green slime—or more precisely Nickelodeon Slime.

Plopped, dropped, and spilled onto the heads and bodies of some of the world's best-known celebrities, slime has been a part of the awards show from the very beginning.

The slime was actually around before the awards ceremony began, appearing on the Nickelodeon game shows *Double Dare* and *Figure it Out.* But green slime made its debut way back in 1979 on a show from Canada called *You Can't Do That on Television*, which was later broadcast on Nickelodeon. And it turns out the slime was created by accident when a bucket of fresh slop was forgotten about and left to sit, turning into a green slime. An actor thought the slop was still fresh and allowed it to be dumped on his head during a skit. The stuff became so popular Nickelodeon decided to market it to the public, offering it for sale to excited boys and girls everywhere—and some not-so-excited parents.

Actor Steve Carell once compared the feeling of being slimed with that of "being sneezed on by a giant." Typically made from a blend of Cream of Wheat, green food coloring, and baby shampoo, it can also contain other ingredients like green Jell-O, applesauce, or vanilla pudding. And if the event calls for the mix to be a little lumpy, bumpy, and gross, you can throw in some cottage cheese.

Over the years sliming celebrities has become a favorite pastime on the Kids Choice Awards, with the audience wondering who is next. Comedian Rosie O'Donnell might be the champion of slime: She has been slimed at least seven times.

A Long Career for a Young Star

In her short career, Selena had already accumulated dozens of awards and accolades over the years including Best Child Actress, Best Young Actress Television, and Outstanding Female Lead in a Comedy Series from various groups. She also received six more awards for her role as Alex Russo on *Wizards of Waverly Place*

The Fan Army

Austin Mahone has Mahomies, One Direction has Directioners, Miley Cyrus has Smilers, and Justin Bieber has his Beliebers. For today's celebrities, having a large "fan army" can often mean the difference between success and failure. Selena Gomez won the Fan Army Award in 2014 because her Selenators beat out other armies in online challenges, including Ariana Grande's Arianators, the Directioners, and Justin Timberlake's JT Superfans.

A fan army is basically a large collection of fans that regularly publicize post and support all the work and endeavors of their favorite celebrity through mass social media activity.

They can be a protective bunch that occasionally needs to be reined in. Lady Gaga found this out when her Little Monsters made online attacks on Katy Perry and Perez Hilton, whom they felt insulted Lady Gaga. Lady Gaga later made a public plea for her Little Monsters to stop attacking her critics.

While it may seem like a new trend, the fan army has actually been around a long time. One of the most notable—the KISS army, created by fans of the rock band KISS—has been active since 1978 and is still going strong.

ranging from Favorite TV actress to Favorite Female Singer from Nickelodeon's Kid Choice. And this doesn't include her prior Teen Choice Awards in 2009 for the made-for-TV movies *Another Cinderella Story* and *The Princess Protection Program* or her Radio Disney Award for Best Female Artist in 2013.

In all, over the previous seven years Selena had won nearly five dozen awards and honors for her work as both an actress and a musician. Not bad at all for a girl from a small town in Texas who dreamed of stardom. At just five years old Selena knew she loved to perform, and by age seven she was convinced it was her true calling. But her dreams might have just remained the stuff of fairy tales if not for the sacrifices of a single mother who put her own dreams on hold in order to give her daughter a better life—a woman who once dreamed of stardom herself.

Selena Gomez: Pop Singer and Actress

Selena Gomez was born and raised in the great state of Texas. Eventually, she would leave home to pursue her dreams.

Chapter 2
Just a Small Town Girl

Amanda Dawn Cornett dreamed of being a star. Born on April 16, 1976 in Dallas, Texas, Amanda was adopted by Debbie Jean Gibson and David Michael Cornett. Amanda's parents made their home in a suburb called Grand Prairie, located about 13 miles (21 kilometers) outside the city.

As their only child, the Cornetts doted on their daughter, who showed an early interest in the theater and performing in front of friends and family. They encouraged her by taking her to auditions in Dallas, where she was cast in several local plays as a child.

Young Love

As she grew older Amanda preferred being called "Mandy." She attended South Grand Prairie High School. In her first year there, she met a boy named Ricardo Gomez—better known to his friends as Rick. The two quickly became an item.

Rick was of Mexican descent, and his extended family was large. It wasn't unusual for his parents, Ricardo and Mary Gomez, to have dozens of cousins staying in the house at any given time. Mandy's roots were Italian. Her family was well known and respected in the community, having lived there for generations. Her mother worked at home cooking big meals for her family and making extra money babysitting local children.

After a while, both sets of parents could tell this was no passing crush for their kids. Rick and Mandy seemed inseparable and had been dating nearly two years. However, no one anticipated just how serious things were about to get.

Life changed forever for the young couple on a typical fall day in 1991, as folks across Grand Prairie were preparing for the holiday season and planning what to eat for Thanksgiving. Mandy, who was just 15 at the time, discovered she was pregnant. Both teenagers knew they were young and the road ahead would be challenging. But with the support of their families, they felt sure they were going to make it work. On July 22, 1992, Rick and Mandy welcomed their new daughter, Selena, into the world.

A Challenging Start to Life

Both Mandy and Rick desperately wanted to finish high school but the odds were against them. Recent statistics show that thirty percent of all teenage girls who drop out of school cite pregnancy and parenthood as key reasons. Only forty percent of teen mothers finish high school,

What's in a Name?

When Mandy and Rick decided to name their daughter Selena, it was in honor of singer Selena Quintanilla-Perez (pictured at right). Known as "The Queen of Tejano Music," Selena was one of the most famous Mexican-American entertainers of the time. She won the Tejano Music Award for Female Vocalist of the Year nine consecutive times and sold more than 60 million albums.

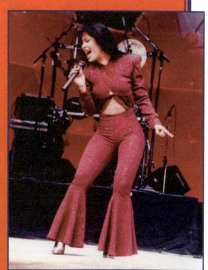

Selena's concerts sold out stadiums, and she was nicknamed "the Mexican Madonna." She was popular not only in the Latin market but internationally. She released the album *Dreaming of You* in 1995, and it was the fastest-selling album by a female artist in pop history.

Born in Lake Jackson, Texas, Selena did not speak fluent Spanish and only learned the language when her popularity began to rise. Her life was cut short at the age of 23 when she was murdered by a former employee and president of her fan club named Yolanda Saldívar on March 31, 1995.

The Governor of Texas at the time was George W. Bush, and he declared her birthday, April 16, Selena Day in Texas. Selena's legacy was also remembered with a postage stamp. A museum created for her stands in Corpus Christi, Texas, a town that also now hosts an annual festival in her honor called *Fiesta de la Flor* (Flower Festival). A movie made about her life was released in 1997 and starred Jennifer Lopez as Selena.

Selena Gomez: Pop Singer and Actress

Gomez's parents were still teenagers when she was born. They named her after their favorite singer.

with less than two percent finishing college by the age of 30. In 1991, when Mandy found herself a new mother, the statistics were even grimmer. However, both sets of new grandparents pledged to help with babysitting duties, so Mandy and Rick were able to stay in school.

Baby Selena lived with her mom and her grandparents, whom she affectionately calls Nana and Papa. "I kind of was raised with my parents and my grandparents," Selena has said. "Nana and papa were like second parents."[1] And when she visited her father, her paternal set of grandparents helped take care of her. They teasingly nicknamed Selena "Flaco," which translates to "slim" in Spanish.

In addition to keeping up in school, Rick and Mandy each had to get a job in order to help support their daughter financially. "It was tough being a teenage parent," Rick said. "That was a big responsibility and a big step that we both had to take."[2] Mandy's responsibilities included getting up in the middle of the night with her infant daughter for feedings—sometimes several times a night—and then making sure she was awake early in the morning to get herself ready for school. "It was tough and you do have to grow up," Mandy said. "I really kind of put forth effort to make sure that I would be able to take care of her and be responsible for her." But keeping up with homework, studying for tests, holding down a job, and caring for her young daughter did take a toll on Mandy. "You are still a child yourself so there are still times that you would make irresponsible decisions,"

Mandy said. "I think the one thing that I truly regret is that I didn't appreciate what being a mother meant at that age."[3]

Both Mandy and Rick realized they had to put Selena first and sacrifice a lot to care for their daughter, but it was a difficult concept for the teenagers to accept. "We were growing up you know and there's only so much you can do right, you can just try your best and hope it works out," Mandy said.[4]

Rick's parents were worried about their son handling all the new responsibilities of fatherhood, but they were very excited to have a new granddaughter and looked forward to taking care of her when he needed help. "When baby Selena was born we were very happy because that was our first granddaughter," Ricardo Sr. said. "We kind of raised her. Selena's father, he was always working. Her mom, Mandy, too was real hard-working when she was a young lady."[5]

A Flair for Performing

As Selena grew older, her paternal grandfather began to notice how much Selena seemed to enjoy performing. "She was one of the kids, not sitting in one place for a while, just always doing something, homemade movies, always acting and singing," he said.[6]

Selena's grandparents encouraged her inherent talent by entering her in beauty pageants and other competitions. When Selena turned three she won first place in a modeling contest.

Just a Small Town Girl

Even as a very small child, Selena loved to perform. Her family recognized immediately that she had talent.

"It was a lot of children, over 400 kids and she came in first place," her grandfather boasted.[7]

With her mother's family having Italian roots and her father coming from a Mexican heritage, Selena grew up in a multicultural environment. "My dad's side it's really all about family...they passed those traditions on to me, I'm really thankful for that," Selena said. "Then on my mom's side it was just more about loving each other and food—because in the south they know how to get some good food."[8]

In keeping with her Mexican heritage, the family celebrated each female family member's fifteenth birthday with a traditional *Quinceañera*. With dozens of older cousins and friends, Selena attended many Quinceañeras as a child and looked forward to having her own someday.

Surrounded by Family and Friends

Selena was raised in the Catholic faith, which meant regular attendance at Sunday mass where she received communion. Her family often went to the park to have a big barbeque after church ended.

Weekends were often filled with family cookouts and get-togethers, but during the week Selena didn't get to see a lot of her parents as they struggled to finish school and hold down jobs.

"It irritates me when people think I live such a special life and that I'm spoiled," said Selena.[9]

She may not have had all the time she desired with her mother and father, but she wasn't lonely because even

The Quinceañera

In the Latin culture, a Quinceañera is a birthday party that celebrates the coming of age of a young woman when she reaches the age of fifteen.

Similar to a "Sweet 16" party, the Quinceañera differs in that it typically begins with a religious ceremony, after which a banquet or reception is hosted with food and music. There is usually a choreographed dance performed by the woman of honor—also called the Quinceañera—and her court of honor, which typically includes siblings and other family members, and close friends.

If the Quinceañera's court is all-female it is called a Dama. If it is all men, it is called a Chambelán, and Escorte, or a Galán. Everyone dresses in their best clothing, and the young woman of honor always dresses in a beautiful gown and often dons a tiara.

The toast given at the banquet, called a "brindis," is a time for everyone to offer their blessings to the Quinceañera. A doll called "The Last Doll" is presented to symbolize the last representation of childhood as the Quinceañera goes forward as a young lady. Sometimes the doll is given to a younger sister.

though she was an only child, she certainly didn't grow up alone. "My grandmother babysat like thirteen kids at once, so I grew up with a bunch of kids around me," Selena said.[10] And being surrounded by other children all the time had its advantages—a lot of friends. "I was a really dramatic kid," said Selena. "My mom would let me run around and make short films and the entire neighborhood would audition for me, just for fun!"[11]

Selena's closest friend was her cousin Priscilla DeLeon. "My cousin Priscilla is as close to a sister as I'm going to get," Selena said. "She's going to be my maid of honor when I get married, and I'm going to be hers."[12] The special bond Selena and Priscilla shared would become very important to Selena when problems began to arise in her parents' marriage.

Chapter 3

Endings and New Beginnings

While other teenagers were going to dances, playing sports, and dreaming of what the future might bring, Mandy and Rick were working multiple jobs and doing homework in any spare time they could find.

As much as her parents tried to help, Mandy was exhausted with the early mornings and late nights involved in caring for a toddler. The carefree days of dates and dances were behind her. She was growing up herself and beginning to realize what was really important to her—and what she wanted her future to look like. Mandy also came to the realization that her feelings for Rick had changed and made the difficult decision to break off their relationship.

Mandy wasn't just thinking about her own feelings. She wanted to set a good example for Selena. "I realized myself there was a bigger world so I didn't want her to think that what you do is go to high school and then graduate, get married, and have kids ... now if that's what you wanted to do great but I also wanted to give her the opportunity to know that there is more out there than this small little town," Mandy said.[1]

The Devastation of Divorce

Selena was just five years old at the time and did not take the news well. At such a young age, she simply couldn't comprehend why her mother no longer wanted to be with her father. All she ever wanted was a family—with a mom and a dad—together.

"I remember when my parents broke up, I didn't understand it," Selena said. "And I blamed my mom a lot because I wanted a family so bad. I wanted to have my dad and my mom together so it was really—it was really hard. I remembered just being really angry with my mom and I still feel really bad for that."[2]

Mandy was well aware of her young daughter's anger. "[Selena] would vent and yell at me and all I could do is just say, 'I'm sorry—but you'll understand someday.'"[3]

Her mother wasn't the only family member to see the toll her parent's divorce took on Selena. "I remember Selena was always like, Priscilla why can't my parents be like yours, and it was really hard," Priscilla said. "And it was really hard to like answer that because I can only imagine what she felt, it was really, really hard."[4]

Endings and New Beginnings

When Selena was five, her parents split up. Mandy (pictured above with Selena) knew she needed to give her daughter more.

The Lone Star State

Texas is the largest of the forty-eight contiguous states. As of the 2013 census, 26,448,193 people made Texas their home. The state is 267,339 square miles and covers 7.4 percent of the United States.

The flags of six nations fly over Texas: Spain, Mexico, France, Republic of Texas, Confederate States, and the United States. From 1836–1845, Texas was an independent nation, and it is the only state that didn't enter the United States by territorial annexation—it was done by treaty.

Before finally becoming part of the United States of America for good, Texas was controlled by several different governments. From 1519–1685 and again from 1690–1821, Spain controlled Texas. France controlled the territory from 1685–1690. It was part of Mexico from 1821–1836 and its own republic from 1836–1845. The United States controlled it from 1845–1861, when it became part of the Confederate States. After the Civil War, the United States regained control.

Texas's nickname—The Lone Star State—was bestowed as a reminder that Texas was once an independent republic and fought for independence from Mexico. Both the Texas state flag and the state seal are emblazoned with the lone star.

One of the state's most popular and well-known sites is The Alamo, in San Antonio. The phrase "Remember the Alamo" originates from the battle that took place here between Texas and Mexico.

Endings and New Beginnings

Selena thought she was losing what she most wanted—a family. However, she still saw her father and grandparents regularly.

Selena's father was also devastated by the end of his marriage. "That pretty much killed me," Rick said. "That hurts so much inside to see my daughter sad."[5]

Traveling a Rough Road

With her marriage to Rick over, Mandy had to make some tough choices. She took Selena and moved from her parent's home into a small apartment in town. Money was extremely tight and young Selena noticed, especially when their car continually ran out of gas, and they had to scrape together change for necessities.

"I remember my mom would run out of gas all of the time and we'd sit there and have to go through the car and get quarters and help her get gas because she never liked to ask my grandparents for money," Selena said. "I remember having a lot of macaroni and cheese."[6]

"I can remember about seven times when our car got stuck on the highway because we'd run out of gas money," Selena said.[7] Mandy remembers the rough times well. "Yeah we might have run out of gas—we did have to walk to the dollar store to get dollar spaghetti and make it. …" Mandy said. "You do the best you can with what you're given."[8]

Even if they ate a lot of pasta, the young mother always made sure she had plenty of it in the house for her daughter to eat. But there were other things in addition to food and shelter that Mandy wanted to provide Selena with—activities and experiences that would enrich the young girl's life. "She saved up to take me to concerts …

Endings and New Beginnings

With little time and even less money, Mandy and Selena endured lean times. Still, Mandy sacrificed a lot for her daughter.

to museums, aquariums, to teach me about the world, about what's real," said Selena.[9]

Living in their own apartment meant new bills to pay, including rent each month. In order to keep up with all the increasing expenses, Mandy worked three jobs. Despite the struggle of raising a daughter and holding down multiple jobs, Mandy knew she had to do even more if she wanted a better life for them both. She needed a better job—a real career that earned more money. For that to happen she knew she needed a better education. So Mandy made the decision to go to college. But the tough times got tougher, at least the first year. Sticking to a daily routine helped her stay on task. "I would get up at 6 in the morning, get her ready for school, drop her off then from there I would go to school and we did that every day," Mandy said. "That was a tough year."[10]

The toughest part for Mandy was feeling like she lost a year of her time with Selena because she was always on the go—to work or to school. Luckily for her, Selena's grandparents continued to help care for their granddaughter during this hectic time.

Selena noticed her mother's continuous absence and at such a young age simply couldn't grasp all the sacrifices her mom was making. And as she grew older, Selena still harbored a lot anger and resentment over her parent's separation, often praying when she was alone that they would reconcile. "I was frustrated that my parents weren't together and never saw the light at the

The Benefits of a College Education

When Selena's mother made the decision to go to college, it wasn't an easy one. In addition to working full time and caring for a young daughter, adding schoolwork to the mix left little if any free time for anything else. But her goal was to have a better life for Selena.

A 2014 study by the New York Federal Reserve confirms her choice was a good one. In fact the report found that "investing in a college degree may be more important than ever before because those who fail to do so are falling further and further behind"—meaning they earn less money and have a hard time finding and maintaining jobs as compared to those who have attended college. Statistics show that having either an associate's degree or a bachelor's degree had an average return of about 15 percent.

Other studies have shown that Americans with a college degree between the ages of 25–32 earned an average of $17,500 more each year than those with just a high school diploma. Over the course of a lifetime, that can mean big money. On average, the person with a bachelor's degree earned $1 million more than the person with just a high school diploma. People with an associate's degree typically earned $325,000 more.

It seems that the sacrifice is well worth the end result.

end of the tunnel where my mom was working hard to provide a better life for me," Selena said.[11]

But there was a light at the end of the tunnel and it was growing brighter—and closer—with each passing moment.

Barney & Friends was a popular children's show that ran on PBS for nearly 20 years.

Chapter 4

A Natural Talent

Like her mother, Selena developed a passion for performing. She loved to write skits and put on plays for the adults. She would recruit her friends and family to audition for various roles, and the dozen or so children her grandmother babysat for came in handy for casting purposes. "I was a really dramatic kid," said Selena. "My mom would let me run around and make short films and the entire neighborhood would audition for me, just for fun!"[1]

Selena was also heavily influenced by her mother's involvement in the theater community. Selena gave her mother a nightly critique of what she could do to improve her scenes and make her performance better. Then she would individually assess the performance of each of Mandy's castmates. "She loved going to rehearsals with me," Mandy said. "One night she started critiquing the actors. I thought, 'Oh boy here we go.'"[2] "I just closed my eyes and thought oh Lord she's going to be an actress."[3]

Her father, Rick, also sensed his daughter's excitement was no passing phase.

Selena absolutely loved to watch her mom practice her lines for a play. She often went to the theater with her and would sit right behind her with her coloring books as her mom prepared for a performance. "My mom did a lot of theater…when she got ready for the show and put on her makeup, I would sit behind her and color and she said, 'You have my lines memorized better than I do!'" Selena said.[4] By the time she was seven, Selena knew she wanted to be an actress. Mandy would always ask her if she was sure—and the answer was always "yes." "I watched my mom do a lot of theater when I was younger and I saw how much passion she had for it," Selena said. "I loved to watch her rehearse. I always wanted to get involved in that."[5]

"She always told her cousin she's going to be famous, she's going to be big," Priscilla said. "She's going to be the next Britney."[6]

Barney

Turns out it wasn't Britney who gave Selena her first big break—it was Barney. Selena was just seven years old when her mom heard about an open casting call for *Barney & Friends*, a children's television show starring America's favorite purple dinosaur, along with his pals Baby Bop and BJ.

Mandy told Selena the audition was on her birthday and asked her if she was interested in going. The answer was a resounding YES! The auditions were close by in

A Natural Talent

Will the Real Barney Please Stand Up?

It's easy to forget that there was a real person under Barney's purple dinosaur costume, but there was. From 1992–2000 it was actor David Joyner. While Barney's voice was performed by someone else, Joyner was the man in the body, dancing, hopping, jumping, and be-bopping.

Just like Selena Gomez, Joyner knew from an early age that he wanted to be performer. When he was a boy he loved to stand in front of the television and mimic the dialogue.

When Joyner auditioned for **Barney**, he didn't get the job at first. The purple dinosaur suit actually went to a young woman. But thankfully for David the woman didn't like the costume and quit, so David was cast as Barney.

The costume was challenging. It weighed approximately 70 pounds (32 kilograms) and temperatures inside could reach over 120 degrees Fahrenheit (49 degrees Celsius).

As Barney, Joyner was on the set of the television show as well as movies and specials, and he often made personal appearances.

Joyner says maneuvering in the suit was difficult. You couldn't be claustrophobic because the only place to see was through the mouth. When the mouth was closed, it was pitch dark inside the suit.

Barney had an army of fans but also some detractors. There was a point when some kids started on the "I hate Barney" bandwagon. Joyner says it hurt his feelings because he knew the message of love everyone on the show was spreading was important and powerful.

another suburb of Dallas called Carrollton. Selena's father was supportive, too. However, he was anxious for his daughter because he knew how much it meant to her. "Selena was so excited about it," Rick said. "I was more nervous than she was."[7]

When Mandy and Selena arrived at what appeared to be an average, ordinary building they saw a huge line of children who clearly had the same dream of stardom. "It was the first thing I auditioned for," Selena said. "I had no experience and no agent and I was standing in line with 1,400 other kids."[8]

By that time, *Barney* had been on television for nearly ten years on television. The show had an audience of two million children watching each episode at its peak of popularity. *Barney* also had "A Day in the Park with Barney," a multimillion-dollar attraction at Universal Studios Florida that drew hundreds thousands of fans every day. *Barney* was big time, and every kid wanted to be on his show.

A New Friend

So Selena and her mom took their spot with more than 1,400 other kids in line and waited. Thinking it might be a while before they reached the front, Mandy was glad she had told her daughter to bring along some coloring books and crayons. As Selena took a seat on the curb to work on a picture, she took notice of the girl in front of them in line.

The girl wore a blue jean jacket and had a big red bow in her hair. She also was coloring while they waited.

A Natural Talent

The talented Selena was chosen from the huge audition to join *Barney's* cast. Her new friend Demi Lovato would join her. In this cast photo, Demi sits on the blue ball and Selena sits on the yellow ball.

The little girl offered to share her crayons with Selena, and Selena readily accepted. The girl's name was Demi Lovato. The two girls would become great friends.

On the Cast of *Barney*

When it was finally Selena's turn to go before the casting director, she turned to her new friend and wished her luck—then went inside with her mother. Soon after returning home from the audition the phone rang at her grandmother's house. "My Nana said I had a phone call and it was someone from *Barney*," Selena said. "They said 'I just want to let you know that you're going to be one of the members of our cast' and I was like 'Are you serious are you serious?'"[9]

Her cousin was in the room at the time and remembers the moment well. "She said 'I got it! I got it! I'm going to be on TV! I'm going to be famous!'"[10]

When the new cast gathered together for their first meeting Selena looked for the friend she had met in line—and sure enough Demi was there. "I was so happy to see her," Selena said.[9] Demi felt the same way. "When we started shooting, Selena was always my favorite," Demi said.[11]

Being part of the cast meant there were scripts to memorize, dances to learn, and songs to practice—and Selena loved every second of it. "I thought it was all glamorous," Selena said. "I thought it was great."[12] Mandy began to notice that her daughter preferred to stay home reading her script rather that going outside and playing with friends.

A Natural Talent

Growing up Demi Lovato

Just twenty-five miles away from Selena Gomez's home in Grand Prairie in another part of Texas, Demi Lovato was also dreaming of being a star. Demi was born on December 28, 2001, in Dallas, Texas. Her mom, Dianna, was an aspiring country singer and a former Dallas Cowboy Cheerleader. Demi has two sisters: Dallas, who is five years older than Demi, and Madison, who was born in 2002. Her parents divorced when Demi was four years old. Demi's father has Mexican and Spanish ancestry; her mother has Irish, Italian, and English roots.

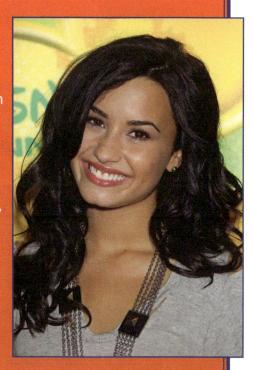

As a youngster, Demi took singing lessons and learned to play the piano and the guitar. She participated in numerous talent shows, winning many of them. She also had the chance to perform with Leann Rimes during a Dallas Cowboys' Thanksgiving Day Half Time Show. But it was when she was cast as Angela on *Barney & Friends* that her acting career began to take off. However, there were some drawbacks to fame—Demi was bullied by classmates just like Selena was. Once, some kids at school even circulated a petition that said "We hate Demi Lovato."

Difficulties Off the Set

In addition to being brand new to the business of filming a television show, which required her to learn terms like "camera right" and "blocking," Selena had something else she had to work very hard to overcome—being shy. "I was very shy when I was little," Selena said.[13]

The film schedule required that Selena miss some school. She was on set three weeks at a time, and then returned to school for a month. But school officials made allowances for her, and she was given the opportunity to take the work she would miss with her to the set. Selena liked the schedule—and the time away from her classes—because actually being at school had become a problem. She was being bullied. Some classmates began leaving notes teasing her about being on *Barney* on her locker and others would sing the classic *Barney* tune "I love you…you love me…" as she walked down the hallway. "I got made fun of a lot," Selena said.[14]

Selena's cousin Pricilla De Leon who attended school with her witnessed much of the teasing. "We had some really mean girls in our school and they would just be like 'oh she's on *Barney*, she's a big baby' and just tease her," Pricilla said. "It hurt her."[15] It got so bad that Selena would cry to her mom and say she didn't want to go to school anymore—which certainly wasn't an option for Mandy.

For two seasons, from 2001–2003, Selena played the role of Gianna on *Barney & Friends*, until at the ripe old age of ten—she was told her role was no longer going to

A Natural Talent

Demi Lovato and Selena Gomez met as kids at an audition, but their friendship has survived. It helps that both are from Texas.

be part of the show. "They said I was getting too old," Selena said. "I cried like a baby when I had to leave."[16]

She knew she wanted to be a star—and had no intention of letting anything derail her. "I wanted more," Selena said. "I was definitely bit by the bug."[17] Selena learned a lot from being a cast member on *Barney*—and she was ready to put that new knowledge to work.

Chapter 5

Leaving Barney Behind

After spending several years of her life as Gianna, life without *Barney & Friends* took some getting used to. "I was just having fun with it, and it turned into something I was really passionate about," Selena said.[1]

As soon as *Barney* was over, Selena cried because she wouldn't get to see Demi as much. But to Selena's surprise, the friendship had only just begun. Demi lived 25 miles away in Colleyville, and since they each had set their sights on a career in acting, their parents decided to work together to focus on honing their acting skills by devoting more time to furthering their careers.

Their friendship blossomed and grew stronger. Not only did they have the same goals and dreams—but they were also both quintessential Texas girls. "We could both sit at a table and eat a jar of pickles, and lemon and salt. It's so weird! In Texas everyone puts lemons on everything," Selena said. "We also say 'y'all.'"[2]

Selena and Demi Lovato stayed close friends. Here they are backstage at the Teen Choice Awards.

Selena didn't have to wait long for more acting jobs to come along—she was quickly cast in several nationally televised commercials for companies like Walmart and TGI Fridays. She also appeared in a commercial for Hasbro with a teddy bear that hugged back.

Acting Lessons

To increase her chances of continued success in the business, Mandy signed her daughter up for acting classes with Dallas-area acting coach Catherine Sullivan. "The person who has the 'it' factor, you can see it in their eyes and Selena had it," Catherine said.[3]

Catherine hosted acting seminars and clinics that Selena regularly attended in Dallas. Her shyness was still an issue. So was her lack of confidence in her abilities, and Catherine noticed. She would tell Selena to chill out, have fun, and not worry so much, but the advice made Selena even more nervous. "Whenever Catherine would give me direction I considered it criticism so I would always freak out and I'd shake and get nervous and sweat and it just got really awkward," Selena said.[4]

It got so bad that Selena would run into the bathroom and refuse to come out until she had calmed down. Catherine did her best to coax her back but Selena was convinced she was doing a terrible job and the tears flowed. "I think a lot of people, especially casting directors, didn't have faith in me, because I would go in not confident, worried, and thinking too much about what they're thinking," Selena said.[5]

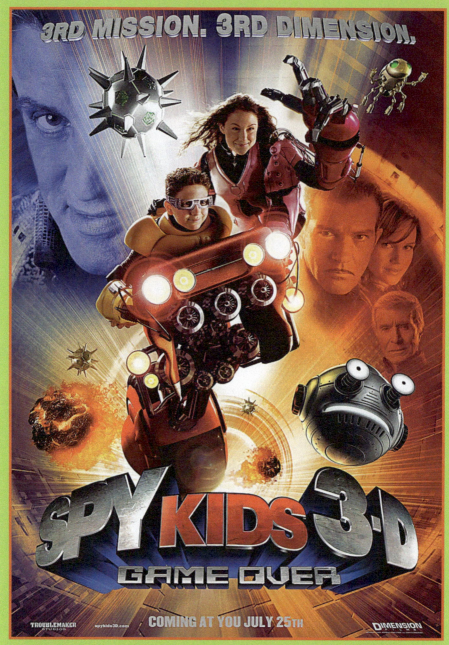

Selena was cast as "Waterpark Girl" in the movie *Spy Kids 3-D: Game Over* (2003).

She was determined and she got focused and then the next time she kicked butt.[6]

Brain Zapped and *Spy Kids*

Selena auditioned for a role in a new television pilot, a children's show called *Brain Zapped*. Eliud George Garcia was the show's director. "Right off the bat I was like 'This kid has got some personality,' but then I heard her read and it was like 'Wow how come this kid is not famous already?,'" Garcia said.[7]

Selena was cast in the lead role as Emily Grace Garcia, a young girl who loved to read. One day she discovers strange goings on at the local library. When she sets out to investigate with her best friend, they are sucked into another world of mystery and imagination.

"Selena had a maturity level about her that is rarely seen in a ten year old, she was determined, she was driven and she just wanted to act," Garcia said.[8]

Selena had a lot of fun working on the project. "It was me, George, and my costar—just us three—running around in libraries… and running around on location," Selena said. "That was really fun and it was really cute."[9]

Unfortunately after filming the pilot, *Brain Zapped* was not picked up by the network. But Selena didn't have time to be too disappointed—she had already been cast in a small part in the movie *Spy Kids 3-D: Game Over*, directed by Robert Rodriguez. She was set to play "Waterpark Girl"—aptly named because her parents owned the water park. The character was wealthy and snobby—it was a fun change of pace for Selena.

Even though her part was very small, the film had some of the biggest stars around in it including; Sylvester Stallone, Salma Hayek, Antonio Banderas, and George Clooney. While much of the movie was filmed on a Hollywood soundstage—Selena was able to stay close to home because her part was filmed at the nearby Schlitterbahn Waterpark Resort in New Braunfels, Texas.

Selena also had the chance to record a song for the film called "Superstar," but in the end it was not included.

Schlitterbahn Waterpark

Much of what you see in the movie *Spy Kids 3-D: Game Over* is created by the magic of special effects, green screens, and computer generated imagery (CGI) in a Hollywood studio. The small role of Waterpark Girl that Selena was cast in was filmed on one of the few real sets right in Texas.

Named "Agua Park" in the movie, the waterpark is actually called Schlitterbahn Water Park, and it is hailed as the world's first water resort. Family owned and operated since 1979, the waterpark has grown immensely over the years—adding new attractions and continuing to attract huge amounts of guests each year. Even though it looks deserted in the movie, the real park employs more than 1,500 seasonal employees, and during its 2000 season it attracted more than 900,000 visitors. It has been featured on several television segments including NBC's *Today Show* and the Travel Channel.

LEAVING *BARNEY* BEHIND

Schlitterbahn Water Park remains a popular summer destination, boasting the world's highest water slide and a giant pool.

A Disney Audition

Playing someone rich and snobby had been fun, but in 2004, 11 year-old Selena found out about a casting call that seemed like a perfect fit for her. Disney was looking for Latina talent—a young girl they could build a show around.

Mandy took Selena to the audition, where she met with casting director Judy Taylor. "Selena was immediately captivating," Taylor said. "You saw glimpses of real potential talent, it was raw but she had great instincts."[10]

After the audition Selena was convinced she had done a terrible job, and her old feelings of insecurity resurfaced. She immediately ran to the bathroom and cried. She had no idea she had actually blown everyone away.

A week later the Disney channel called and wanted to fly her out to do a testing in Los Angeles. It would be Selena's first time on a plane, and she studied the script the entire plane ride over. The show was called *Stevie Sanchez*, and it was intended to be a potential spinoff of Lizzie McGuire—which just happened to be Selena's favorite show. "Of course, I worshiped the Disney Channel when I was younger," Selena said. "*Lizzie McGuire, Suite Life*—I wanted to be like Lizzie."[11]

At the audition, Selena yet again felt she had bombed the reading and went to the lobby and cried. But Disney disagreed. Gary Marsh, then president of entertainment for Disney Channels Worldwide, saw something very

Latina vs. Hispanic

A Latina is defined as a woman or girl of Latin American origin or descent. A Latin American male is called a Latino. You may have also heard the term *Hispanic*. Latino and Hispanic are often used interchangeably, but they don't actually mean the same thing.

Hispanic originally denoted a relationship to ancient Hispania and was first used as a term in the United States census in the 1970s. The term was intended to include people from Spain, Mexico, Cuba, Central America, and South America. So, a native of Spain residing in the United States is a Hispanic.

The decision was made not to use the word Latina/Latino in the early census because it could also include Europeans of Latin origin, and the government wanted accurate numbers so it could implement laws to assist this growing and increasingly discriminated-against population.

In 2000, the use of *Latino* began to be used in the census as a way to include the ever-changing and constantly-evolving mix of cultures.

The term is more appropriately applied to those who come from communities of Latin-American origin. A person from Brazil is a Latino/Latina but is not Hispanic.

Both Hispanic and Latina/Latino were meant to indicate ethnicity as opposed to race but are often used interchangeably.

special in Selena—something real and genuine—he loved her big personality.

Selena won the role. She was so excited she felt for the first time like she was really going to make it in show business.

Disappointment

Meanwhile, back home Selena was cast to play a part in one of her grandmother's favorite shows, *Walker, Texas Ranger*. She would also appear in a made-for-TV movie called *Trial by Fire*, in the role of Julie.

Everything seemed to be going so well for Selena, but bad news was just a phone call away. *Stevie Sanchez* hadn't been picked up for production. The show and Selena's leading role were gone. It was heartbreaking news and Selena, and her family were extremely disappointed.

But Gary Marsh had made a promise—he told Selena he would find the right show for her. He wasn't about to let her get away. "It's a little bittersweet when you find somebody that talented and you feel you failed because you haven't put her in the right vehicle," Marsh said. "But I wanted to assure her that we would find the right vehicle for her, no matter what it took."[12]

Chapter 6

DISNEY DREAMS

Sometimes one person can make all the difference. In Selena's case, Gary Marsh was that person. He believed in her ability to be a major star and made it his mission to make her part of the Disney family. "I knew Selena was incredibly special. She was not going to get away from us," Marsh said. "Whoever had to be convinced of that at the time, I made it my business to convince them."[1]

And convince them he did. Selena landed her first major role as a guest star playing "Gwen" in *The Suite Life of Zack & Cody* on the Disney Channel. The show followed the adventures of identical twins Zack and Cody, who live in a hotel. It also happened to be one of her favorite shows.

For Selena, it was surreal being on the set. She was used to watching the characters on television, and here she was with the very people she was a fan of.

It was all part of Marsh's plan—to get Selena the experience she needed in front of the camera on an established show. In addition to it being her first big role, she also experienced another first on the set—her first kiss. In the episode, Selena played the role of Cody's girlfriend, who is cast along with Zack in a play. The script calls for the two to kiss—so they did. And that's how Selena's very first kiss took place—in front of four cameras, an audience, and her mother—with actor Dylan Sprouse.

Hannah Montana

Soon after her role on *The Suite Life*—and in keeping with Marsh's plan to get her more experience—Selena was cast in a guest spot on another well-known Disney Channel show—*Hannah Montana*. She played the role of the conniving Mikayla, Hannah's nemesis. It became a recurring role in season 2, and Selena appeared in three episodes.

All her hard work paid off, and in 2006 Selena got a call that Disney wanted her to come back to Los Angeles to audition for two new Disney Channel live-action new pilots. One was called *The Amazing Hannigans* and the other was *Housebroken*, a spinoff of *The Suite Life of Zack and Cody*.

Changes at Home

Selena's career wasn't the only one taking off. Mandy began making a name for herself, as well. She worked as a special makeup effects artist on the set of the 2003

Selena appeared in three episodes of the popular Disney show *Hannah Montana*.

film *Pale Blue Moon*, and in 2004 she was hired on as assistant director and unit production manager for *Blue October: Argue with a Tree*. In 2006, Mandy worked as a coordinator on animated projects, including *Ant Bully*.

She was also in love. Several years earlier, Mandy had begun a relationship with a man named Brian Teefey, and on May 18, 2006 she became Mandy Teefey when they exchanged marriage vows. It was hard on Selena when Mandy first introduced her to Brian because she still held out hope that her parents would someday reconcile. But over time, she came to love Brian. She could see how much her mother loved him and how happy he made her.

Later that year, Mandy began her own production company called "July Moon Productions" and made her husband the vice-president. Mandy named the company after her daughter—Selena means "moon" in Greek and

What Ever Happened to Arwin?

Gary Marsh, then president of entertainment at Disney Channels Worldwide, knew when he cast Selena Gomez as a lead in two live-action pilots Disney was producing that one of them would not see the light of day because they only had room for one show in the lineup.

In 2006, Disney announced the pilots for two new shows. One of them went on to mega success as *Wizards of Waverly Place,* and the other—not so much.

Originally titled *Housebroken*—and then changed to *Arwin*—the show was a spinoff of *The Suite Life* that focused on the character of Arwin the handyman, played by Brian Stepanek. In the pilot, Arwin moves in with his sister to help take care of her children.

Selena was cast as Alexa, along with current pop star Jasmine Villegas as Lidia and Samantha Droke, who was set to play the part of Summer. Droke later appeared with Selena in *The Princess Protection Program*.

The cast filmed the pilot in late 2006, and the production extended into February 2007. That December Disney announced it would not be picking up the show, and the pilot never aired.

Disney Dreams

Selena auditioned for a spinoff of one of her favorite shows, *The Suite Life of Zack and Cody*, starring Dylan and Cole Sprouse.

she was born in July. The three of them shared a home in Texas, along with several dogs.

A Picked-Up Pilot

Back in Hollywood, Disney's Gary Marsh had made the decision to cast Selena in both pilots because he knew they only had room in the scheduling lineup for one show—and he wasn't about to lose Selena again.

When Selena got the call that she was cast in both shows, she was beyond excited. Sure enough, *The Suite Life* spinoff was cut, so Selena accepted a role as Julia on *The Amazing Hannigans*, a show focused on two teenage siblings living in New York City. The siblings are named Jordan and Julia, and they also happened to be wizards. But studio executives soon decided to change the name of the show to *The Amazing O'Malleys*. So instead of Julia, Selena would now be Brooke O'Malley. It didn't matter to Selena what her name would be—as long as the show went on.

Winning the lead in a brand new Disney show meant commuting to Los Angeles was no longer an option. Selena would need to make the move to California. Knowing Hollywood was fickle and acting jobs came and went easily, Brian decided to stay behind with the dogs just in case the series wasn't picked up and Selena and Mandy needed to return to Texas. He would go only when they were sure the move would be permanent.

Make It or Break It—The Pilot Episode

You can have a great idea for a story and put it in writing. You can craft a script with interesting and catchy dialogue. You can find the perfect actors to fill each role in the cast—but even if you do all this—you have only completed the first few steps in creating a successful television sitcom.

When television executives have three shows they really like but only have room for one in the seasonal lineup, the pilot can be a major deciding factor. A pilot is a stand-alone episode used to sell the show to a television network. It serves as a testing ground. Could it be successful as a series? Does it have the right elements? Is the cast in sync? TV executives have to look at a wide range of factors in their decision-making process. The results could range from an order for additional episodes, a change in cast or concept, or complete rejection.

Only about a quarter of all American television pilots are actually picked up for a series, and those that don't make it are almost never seen publicly.

Before anything is decided, the pilot typically goes through a series of evaluations including focus groups of random members of the public who give their honest opinions after a screening. Gary Marsh, now Chief Creative Officer of Disney Channels Worldwide, said he spends a lot of time talking to, listening to and watching the reaction of kids in their focus groups. "Sometimes it will be eight to 10 kids in a room, and we'll show them an episode and then sit with them for an hour and a half asking what worked and what didn't, " Marsh said in an interview with the *Hollywood Reporter*. "There's also a huge quantitative research effort, which is going out online to 300 to 500 kids at a time with a show and then doing a vote of was this funny or not funny or who is their favorite character."

California, Here We Come

Selena and her mother packed for Los Angeles—and said their goodbyes. It was very hard for Selena to leave her father, her grandparents, her cousins, and her friends. Her father was a nervous wreck, but he knew Selena had worked so hard for this and he didn't want to do anything to get in her way now.

Leaving Texas was one of the hardest things Selena ever had to do. "It was almost a test of how badly I really wanted to pursue acting. Which I did, there was no question in my mind that I wanted to come out here and do this," Selena said. "But it was really tough to leave my friends behind."[2]

One of her best friends, Demi Lovato, had also tried out for Disney but was not cast. "There were tears, crying and everything," Selena said. "We both auditioned for Disney. She didn't get it. I did. We've had those moments, but we're so proud of each other that it doesn't affect us."[3]

However, Demi's older sister, Dallas, who was also trying to establish a career as an actress was cast in a small role playing "Rachel" in the same show Selena would be starring on, *The Amazing O'Malleys*! So Demi Lovato, along with her mother and sisters Dallas and Madison, decided to move to L.A. The move would also give Demi the opportunity to attend more auditions. Madison was just a toddler at the time.

Mandy and Selena packed the car and set off for L.A. Selena cried much of the way. Once there, they moved into a loft apartment in the downtown area.

Disney Dreams

Although it was difficult to adjust to her mother's boyfriend at first, Selena grew to love Brian by the time he married Mandy.

It was difficult to get used to the big city, and Selena would often fall asleep in tears. But during the day—when she was working on set—she was the happiest she'd ever been.

Working on the pilot was a lot of work—but also a lot of fun. Selena had gotten used to things changing quickly in Hollywood—and so she wasn't that surprised when the name of the show was changed again—to *Wizards of Waverly Place.*

Chapter 7

THERE'S A NEW WIZARD IN TOWN

Change is constant in Hollywood. When *Wizards of Waverly Place* became the official name of Selena's new series, other changes came with it. Dallas Lovato's part was cut, along with several others in the cast.

Selena was asked to sing the show's theme song, and her character would now be named Alex Russo. Also, instead of one brother, she would have two. Actor David Henrie would play her brother Justin Russo, and Jake T. Austin would play her brother Max Russo. Joe Jonas from the Jonas Brothers auditioned for the role of Justin Russo and was under serious consideration before Disney decided to go with Henrie.

It was an awkward feeling at first. All the young actors were relatively new to the business. But as they got to know each other, everyone bonded and became close. You might even say they became—a family.

Jennifer Stone played Harper Finkle, Alex's best friend. "We were just two little girls that were so excited to have a job," Stone said. "It was so thrilling it's one of those once-in-a-lifetime experiences where you all just get along. It became like a second family."

Successes for Disney

Wizards of Waverly Place premiered October 12, 2007. Disney's then president of entertainment Gary Marsh was thrilled. "When *Wizards* hit it was clear that we had found another superstar," Marsh said. "The audience responded to Selena in ways we could have only imagined."[1]

Once on hiatus (break) from the show, Selena signed on to do two other projects for the Disney Channel—the made-for-TV movies *Another Cinderella Story* and *The Princess Protection Project,* which paired Selena up with her friend of eight years, Demi Lovato.

They had a great time filming together. The only challenging part was being directed to argue so much when they were in character because in reality the friends had barely had a disagreement. *The Princess Protection Project* ended up being one of Disney Channel's highest-rated movies.

After such success, studio executives were anxious to have Selena focus on a music career, but Selena had different ideas. While she definitely wanted to do music, it wasn't the right time for her. She wanted to focus on

There's a New Wizard in Town

Selena starred in a successful new show for the Disney Channel, playing Alex Russo in the *Wizards of Waverly Place*.

her show, building a fan base, and making the most of what she already had.

So when Selena was offered the lead role in *Camp Rock*, she turned it down and her best friend Demi was cast instead alongside The Jonas Brothers—a popular band consisting of Nick, Joe, and Kevin—who had starred in their own Disney Channel series.

Even though The Jonas Brothers and Demi Lovato were playing sold-out arenas after the movie's release, Selena knew she had made the right decision for herself—even if some Disney executives disagreed.

Famous First Boyfriend

Turning down the role in *Camp Rock* didn't keep her from getting to know the Jonas Brothers—especially one brother in particular—Nick. The two began spending time together after she appeared in a Jonas Brothers music video for the single "Burnin' Up." They went out together and she started showing up backstage at his concerts. It was at one of those concerts that she met Taylor Swift, who was dating Joe Jonas at the time. The two became good friends and began to keep in touch.

"Taylor and I dated Jonas brothers together. We met when she was 18. I was 15 or 16. She was so great to me. Then we became best friends," Selena said. "She would fly out to see me when I was going through something really hard. We'd eat a lot of fattening food and vent."[2]

Nick had just ended a long relationship with Miley Cyrus (star of *Hannah Montana*), and speculation began to rise in the media that a feud between the two girls

There's a New Wizard in Town

Selena became good friends with the Jonas Brothers, even casually dating Nick Jonas.

was brewing. It was the first time Selena began to see the negative side of publicity.

But Selena downplayed the significance of the relationship. "I had my first 'boyfriend' [Nick Jonas], which wasn't really a boyfriend, at 14, 15," Selena said. "You're young and you don't know how to be."[3] The relationship soon ended.

Turning to Her Music

Back on the set of *Wizards*, Selena felt safe and secure. Her television family gave her a sense of comfort and protection. "My mom laughs at me all the time because we're constantly in touch with one another off the set, we're always calling," Selena said. "They're always there for me, and its torture when I can't see them every day. We do fight like brothers and sisters sometimes, but mostly we play around and joke around. I don't have any real life siblings so this way I can have brothers." [4]

In 2008 Selena finally felt it was time to give music her attention, and at age 16 she signed with Hollywood records. Around the same time the Disney Channel was planning an original movie based on the *Wizards of Waverly Place* series, and a portion of it was to be filmed in Puerto Rico. It was the perfect spot for Selena to begin working on songs for her debut album.

Selena became good friends with music superstar Taylor Swift when they both dated Jonas Brothers. Their friendship has outlasted both of the romantic relationships!

There's a New Wizard in Town

In the animated film *Horton Hears a Who!*, Selena lent her voice to the character of Helga, the mayor's daughter.

Wizards of Waverly Place: The Movie debuted on August 28, 2009, with 11.4 million viewers watching the premiere. That made it the second-most-viewed Disney premiere in the United States, after *High School Musical 2*. *Wizards of Waverly Place: The Movie* also took home an Emmy Award in 2010 for "Outstanding Children's Program."

Branching Out

Disney had been good to Selena, but they weren't the only ones who could see her star power. Selena was cast to voice the part of Helga, the mayor's daughter, in the animated movie *Horton Hears a Who!* She was also offered one of the title roles in the major motion picture *Ramona and Beezus* and readily accepted. Filming took place in Vancouver, Canada. The minute Selena met her costar Joey King, she knew they would become

From the Written Page to the Silver Screen

Before the movie *Ramona and Beezus*, starring Selena Gomez and Joey King, even began filming the sisters already had an established following—sisters Ramona and Beezus that is. That's because the movie was based on a book that's actually called *Beezus and Ramona*—as well as seven other books in the "Ramona" books series of children's novels by Beverly Cleary. Since 1955, when the first book was published, readers have been enjoying the adventures and humorous antics of the irrepressible Ramona.

Many of Hollywood's biggest hits started out as a book first, including *Twilight*, *The Hunger Games*, *The Hobbit*, *The Fault in Our Stars*, *Divergent*, *Alexander and the Terrible, No Good, Very Bad, Horrible Day*, *The Maze Runner*, *Harry Potter*, and many others.

It can be a slippery slope to make a successful transition from page to screen. The first step is adapting it for the big screen by writing a screenplay. The written word can't be translated precisely to film—edits must be made to keep the action in the required time constraints of a movie, and that means cutting out whole scenes in order to make it work.

When movie executives adapted the well-known Dr. Seuss tale *The Lorax*, the movie differed so much from the book most people thought it was a sequel.

There are many other vocal disgruntled fans that loved a book—but hated the movie version. For instance some fans of the book *Life of Pi* by Yann Martel were excited to see how director Ang Lee would make certain aspects of the book work and found out he didn't—he just left them out completely. And some folks who read *Stand by Me*, a novella by Stephen King, were surprised to find a completely different ending in the movie than what happened in the book.

close. They even began to feel like real sisters. Joey said that Selena looked after her like a big sister, and Selena admitted she could not have gotten through the film without her.

Joey wasn't the only new friend Selena made in Canada. Another young popular star was in town filming another movie on a vastly different topic than her family-friendly flick. This one was about vampires and werewolves—and a girl who loved them. It was called *The Twilight Saga: New Moon* and one of its stars fell for Selena.

They happened to meet when one of the movie's other stars, Kristen Stewart, was staying at the same hotel Selena was in. Taylor Lautner would come to the hotel to visit Stewart and often ran into Selena in the hotel lobby. They began talking and started to spend time together.

"He is so sweet. Taylor has made me so happy. I didn't know I could be that happy. You probably see it in the pictures! I'm like smiling so big," Selena told reporters. The couple would go to lunch and dinner—but always with paparazzi in tow. "We literally just wanted to hang out, go bowling and stuff, and it went a little too far, I think. People were getting a little crazy about us," Selena said.[5]

The attention got to be too much and the couple decided it was best to go their separate ways. But it's a time Selena remembers fondly. "I went to Vancouver thinking I was going to focus on my work, but instead

The Great White North—the New Hollywood?

While Selena was in Vancouver filming *Ramona and Beezus* she met the cast of Twilight—who were also in town filming *The Twilight Saga: New Moon*. In fact many production companies are choosing Canada over the United States when it comes time to filming. Do you ever wonder why?

After all Ramona and Beezus live in Portland, Oregon, and the folks from *Twilight* are from Forks, Washington. But in fact every year thousands of film and television productions choose Canada as their film location—because it can pass for locations in America—and the main reason—it's a lot less expensive.

Vancouver doubles for the Middle America states—Toronto is used in place of New York City and Calgary passes as the western states. Some well-known movies that might have fooled you include *Good Will Hunting*, which takes place in Boston but was filmed in Toronto. *My Big Fat Greek Wedding* was set in Chicago and filmed in Toronto. *The Incredible Hulk* took place in New York City but was filmed in Toronto, and the *Mean Girls* lived in Illinois, but the film was shot in Toronto.

Some well-known American television series were also shot in Canada including *21 Jump Street*, *MacGyver*, *The X Files*, and —currently—*Once Upon a Time*, *Supernatural*, and *Arrow* still film there.

With the current favorable currency exchange rate, Canada's reign as a premier location for film and television doesn't seem to be ending anytime soon.

There's a New Wizard in Town

Selena and her co-star Joey King attended the premiere of *Ramona and Beezus* in New York City.

I got to meet him, and it ended up being the best thing ever," Selena said.[6]

Back at home, *Wizards of Waverly* place had been a fan favorite for four seasons and 106 episodes. On Friday, January 6, 2012, *Wizards of Waverly Place* aired its one-hour series finale; "Who Will Be the Family Wizard?" with a viewing audience of nearly 10 million. It was the most-watched finale for a Disney Channel Original Series.

Chapter 8

And Then There Was Justin

It all started off innocently enough. In 2010 Selena's mom Mandy, who was also working as her manager, received a call from the manager of another young performer. It turned out that superstar singer Justin Bieber wanted to meet Selena—and Mandy agreed.

The two became close friends, spending a lot of time together. But they insisted there was no romance—with Selena referring to herself as more of a big sister to him. However later that same year, the two were spotted holding hands while having breakfast in Philadelphia.

Once rumors of a relationship began to circulate, Selena and Justin became a prime target and focus of the rabid paparazzi hoping to snap a photo of the two teens together. Then on New Year's Day 2011, Selena and Justin were photographed kissing on the balcony of a beach home.

Selena Gomez: Pop Singer and Actress

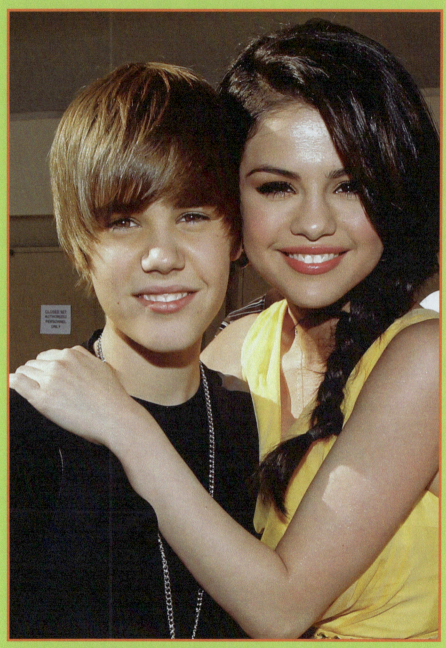

Selena has had an on-again off-again relationship with fellow young talent Justin Bieber.

And Then There Was Justin

On February 27, 2011 there was no mistaking the fact that Selena and Justin were a couple as they arrived on the red carpet hand in hand at the *Vanity Fair* after party following the 2011 Oscars in Hollywood. Just days earlier, Justin had ordered multiple trucks filled with flowers from a local florist so he could fill Selena's house with them. Fans coined the nickname "Jelena" for the couple. But the young stars continued to be vague about their relationship in public.

In June, at the age of 19, Selena appeared on *Fox & Friends* for an interview to promote her upcoming movie *Monte Carlo*, a romantic comedy about three girls who travel around Europe. The movie was set to debut July

Justin Bieber

Justin Bieber was born on March 1, 1994, in London, Ontario. He is the only child of Jeremy Jack Bieber and Patricia Mallette who were never married. Justin learned to play piano, drums, guitar, and the trumpet at a young age. He also showed an early talent for singing. After entering a local singing competition and coming in second place, his mother posted a video of the performance in which he sang Ne-Yo's "So Sick" on YouTube. Family and friends loved it, so she continued to update the account with more videos of Justin singing.

Quite by accident, a marketing executive by the name of Scooter Braun came across Justin's videos while looking for someone else and he liked what he saw. Braun tracked the boy down and signed him to a recording contract with Raymond Braun Media Group, a company Braun ran with the well-known singer Usher.

11 and Selena was on a media tour, visiting malls and connecting with fans. She was also talking up the release of her third album, *When the Sun Goes Down*. The topic of Justin Bieber was brought up and Selena was asked directly if she and Justin were in a relationship. Selena kept her cool and simply responded that it was nice to have someone who understands what you are going through.

Justin was equally reserved when he appeared on television talk show *The View* on November 23, 2011. Clearly not wanting to address the relationship in any great detail, cohost Elisabeth Hasselbeck was able to get him to admit they were dating. "Well here's the thing uh you're putting me on the spot here," Justin said. "People know that we are dating and stuff but I like to keep certain privacy—I have to have something that's special to me that I don't share with everyone else so I can have something for myself."[1]

But the questions about his relationship with Selena kept coming and small amounts of information about his feelings were coming out. In an interview with E! online Justin referred to Selena as his "special friend" and on *The Ellen Degeneres Show* he admitted Selena has "very kissable cheeks."

Stress Takes a Toll on Selena's Health

For Selena, denials over a serious relationship with Justin didn't seem to stop his more intense fans from sending her hate mail—and even threatening her life. "It's hard," Selena said. "It hurts, it really does. I don't feel like I'm

And Then There Was Justin

Gomez starred in the 2011 film *Monte Carlo*. She also contributed a song, "Who Says."

SELENA GOMEZ: POP SINGER AND ACTRESS

The Green Room

Selena Gomez has been a guest on *The Ellen DeGeneres Show* numerous times. She's also sat down for chats with *The Tonight's Show*'s Jay Leno and Jimmy Fallon, *Late Night with David Letterman*—and countless others.

In 2014 while waiting backstage to go on *Ellen*, Selena sent a tweet out to her followers sharing some photos of her in the "Green Room" getting last minute makeup touches and indulging on chips, pretzels, and soda. But many of her fans might have wondered, "What is a green room?"

The Green Room is a room that serves as a waiting room for guests who are going to appear on a television show. Almost every interview-style or news show has a Green Room. But why green? Well, that just happened to be the color most were painted over the years and it caught on.

While each Green Room is unique they usually offer comfortable seating, and food—which can be simple snacks or extravagant spreads and drinks. There are also typically mirrors, makeup, hair products, and other sundries. A television monitor broadcasting the program being taped is usually on so guests can see what's happening on stage.

doing anything wrong. I've been best friends with him for a very long time. It does hurt my feelings a lot but I try not to focus on it. I have a strong family and great fans."[2]

But the stress of it all may have taken its toll on Selena. On June 10, after appearing on *The Tonight Show* with Jay Leno—during which she was asked if her mom liked Justin Bieber and she said "yes, he passed the

And Then There Was Justin

Just a few months after being hospitalized for treatment of minor health issues, Selena was back on *The Tonight Show With Jay Leno*.

test"—Selena was rushed to the hospital because she had a severe headache and was feeling nauseous.

She canceled a few scheduled appearances in order to regain her strength. Her hospital stay and talk of feeling nauseous sparked a new wave of panic on social media—with fans and detractors alike speculating on whether she was pregnant—she wasn't. Later she blamed the issue on being malnourished and eating too much junk. "The problem is I don't eat right. I love everything that's possibly not good for me," Selena said. "I love M&Ms, Kit Kats, Snickers and Goobers at the movies."[3]

For proof of this fact, a fan has to look no further than the famous secret handshake (The Kit Kat Bar Shake) Selena and Demi have been doing since they were little girls. They revealed it on their You Tube channel in 2008. The chant that accompanies the handshake is a tribute to their beloved Kit Kat Candy Bar.

More Stress

In November 2011, Selena Gomez took to the social media site Twitter to joyfully announce that her mother was pregnant with a girl. That same month Justin was named in a paternity suit—and rumors of a breakup began to swirl, but they were still seen out together.

Sadly the next month on December 16, Mandy was rushed to the hospital, where she suffered a miscarriage and Selena's sister who was to be named Scarlett was gone. Justin cancelled several performances in order to go to the hospital—and show his support for Selena during this tragic time.

And Then There Was Justin

In November 2012 the couple took a break from dating citing their busy schedules as the reason but by December they were seen vacationing together at a ski lodge. Rumors of a breakup began to pick up traction in January 2013—especially after an appearance by Selena on *The Late Show with David Letterman* to promote her newest movie *Spring Breakers*, costarring James Franco. During the interview Letterman asked if she had a boyfriend. "No I'm single, Selena said. Then she quickly added, "I'm so good."[4]

When Letterman relayed a story about how he once made Justin Bieber cry, Selena replied "Well that makes two of us."

Gomez took on a more mature role in the 2012 movie *Spring Breakers*, in which four college students go on a wild spring break.

Selena Gomez: Pop Singer and Actress

After her emotional performance at the 2014 American Music Awards Selena broke down in tears. The song she sang, "The Heart Wants What it Wants," may have been written about Justin Bieber.

A Final Break?

But by April Selena had traveled to Norway, where she was photographed embracing Justin. The couple seemed to be back on for the next few months—with photos of the happy couple kissing and hugging appearing in magazines on a daily basis. However in July 2013 during an interview with Ryan Seacrest, Selena said she was single.

In January 2014, Justin posted a photo on social media of the two in an embrace with the caption "Love the Way You Look at Me." The photo has nearly 2 million views. In June he posted another photo with the caption "Our Love is Unconditional," which he later deleted.

Selena eventually decided to call it quits amid rumors of infidelity on Justin's part that were reinforced with pictures taken by paparazzi—not to mention the flirty photos he posted of himself with other women.

During the 2014 American Music Awards at L.A.'s Nokia Theatre on Sunday, November 23, Selena gave a highly emotional performance of her new song "The Heart Wants What It Wants" from her greatest hits collection *For You*. Many have speculated the song was written about Justin Bieber. As she performed the song, the shadow of a man similar in stature to Justin appeared behind her as she belted out the song's lyrics. When she finished the song, Selena wept onstage.

Selena Gomez: Pop Singer and Actress

In addition to UNICEF, Selena has volunteered for many charities, including a pediatric AIDS foundation benefit sponsored by Disney.

Chapter 9
MORE TO LIFE THAN FAME AND FORTUNE

In addition to becoming a fan favorite of millions of young girls for her celebrity status, Selena Gomez's charitable work has garnered the attention and admiration of people everyone. She's already made humanitarian missions to the Democratic Republic of Congo, Ghana, and Chile to witness firsthand the struggles that result from war and poverty.

UNICEF

When Selena was just 17, she was appointed a UNICEF Ambassador in September 2009 becoming the youngest person to ever serve. UNICEF was founded in 1947 and stands for United Nations International Children's Emergency Fund. Their goal is improving the lives of children everywhere by providing access to clean water, food, medicines, immunizations, and education. Since taking on the position of ambassador, Selena has worked to save lives threatened by starvation and inadequate nutrition in the Sahel region of West and Central Africa.

After visiting UNICEF's Emergency Operation Centre in New York, she learned about their various emergency programs and how crucial social media is in making today's youth aware of important social issues.

With millions of followers on her various social media sites—she was able to promote an international call for help—called "Sound the Alarm," in order to raise money to help malnourished children. Selena also recorded a public service announcement aimed at young adults asking for small donations to make a big difference.

In 2012, Selena and her band The Scene hosted a charity concert to benefit UNICEF and raised $20,000 for the organization in one sold-out show.

"Giving back has always been important to me. This concert allows me to connect with my fans in person, which is one of the best parts of my job, and to raise money for important causes at the same time," Selena said. "I can't think of anything I would enjoy doing more."[1]

Four-Legged Friends

Having a huge fan base on social media came in handy again when Selena decided to do something to help stray dogs. As someone who loves animals and has five dogs herself, Selena was shocked when she visited Puerto Rico

A Helping Hand

It's one thing to pledge money to a cause you care about—and that money can do wondrous things—but it's something else entirely to physically go to an area beseeched by poverty and drought. A place where violence can be sudden and education is limited. It takes courage to go outside your comfort zone and leave the comfort of everything you're used to behind. But that's exactly what Selena Gomez did in 2009 when Selena made her first official field mission as a UNICEF Ambassador on a trip to Ghana to see firsthand the vital work UNICEF performs on behalf of that country's vulnerable children. Then in January 2011 she traveled to Valparaiso, Chile for a visit with the children and families being helped by "Programa Puente."

Selena often raised money for causes by eliciting support from fans and doing concerts to benefit the charity. But this time she wanted to see firsthand the difference a program like those supported by UNICEF can make.

Programa Puente—which translates to Bridge Program in English—helps to promote early childhood education and development, parenting skills, and other issues important to a family's well-being. "UNICEF is helping Chilean families get out of poverty, prevent violence within the home and promote education," Selena said. "To witness firsthand these families' struggles, and also their hope and perseverance, was truly inspiring."[2]

Pets, particularly dogs, play an important role in Selena's life. She has contributed time and money to several rescue groups.

and saw the number of stray dogs wandering along the local beaches. "It broke my heart, going to work every day and not being able to do anything," Selena said.[3]

On a return trip to the area while filming the *Wizards of Waverly Place* movie, she decided to do something to help. Selena and her mom tried to find a group they could partner with and found Island Dog, a charitable group that rescues dogs in the Caribbean. She put the word out on social media about the group's mission and then hosted a fund-raising event in San Juan that raised $17,000.

"We were vaccinating the dogs and rubbing oil on their backs so they don't get fleas," Selena said. "We got to feed them and play with them. It was sweet and heartbreaking at the same time."[4] Selena even took one lucky pup home and named him Chazz. "He's adorable!," Selena said. "He got hit by a car and had a broken leg. We kept him in our hotel room and gave him a bath and fed him, and ended up flying him to our house. You feel good about the little things you do, like feeding or bathing a dog," she says. "It's empowering."[5]

It's Not Easy Being Green

Selena's charitable reach has been wide as she continues to support a wide variety of different causes for people, animals, and amphibians.

After learning about the severe consequences related to the disappearance of amphibians around the world and its impact on world ecology, Selena even made a Public Service Announcement with Kermit the Frog in

Selena Gomez poses with former Nickelodeon star Miranda Cosgrove at the Target Presents Variety's Power of Youth event. The busy star always makes time to volunteer her money and time.

order to promote conservation efforts aimed at solving the amphibian crisis.

House Calls

Selena has also volunteered her time as a runway model to St. Jude Children's Research Hospital, where she joined other celebrities in raising more than $1 million.

She also joined with the Ryan Seacrest Foundation in launching "The Voice" in the Children's Hospital of Philadelphia. The program is intended to offer an artistic outlet for sick and injured children and Selena got the opportunity to sing "Who Says" with a 1-year-old girl awaiting a heart transplant.

She joined fellow Disney Channel superstar Joe Jonas in "The Voice" program on behalf of the Ryan Seacrest Foundation. Jonas and Gomez enjoyed working with sick children in a space where they can try their hand at TV, radio, and new media. "It's definitely one of my favorite parts of my job," Selena said. "Being able to do this is nice and humbling."[6]

Other Volunteer Organizations

Selena also volunteers for Rosie's Theater Kids, a group whose goal is to provide enrichment to children through arts education by offering workshops in drama, dance, and music.

And she recorded a series of public service announcements to encourage safe driving.

Selena also volunteers her time visiting schools and promoting support for "A Day Made Better"—an organization that raises money each year to provide more than 1,000 teachers with $1,000 each so they can purchase supplies for students in class.

She lent her talents as a narrator to 10x10 and their production of "Girl Rising" in support of the group's worldwide effort promoting girl's education.

Other charitable organizations Selena supports or volunteers for include Alliance For Children's Rights, the Cystic Fibrosis Foundation, Elton John AIDS Foundation, Free the Children, Malala Fund, Stand Up to Cancer, and Teen Cancer America.

Selena has also brought awareness to a condition she actually suffers from. In her late teens she was diagnosed

Glamour Magazine named Selena its Woman of the Year in 2012. Her volunteer work was a factor in winning the prestigious award. The magazine recognized Selena's rare gifts—particularly for her age.

What Is Lupus?

The symptoms of Lupus are varied. Headaches, being extremely tired, fever, swelling, hair loss, anemia, fingers turning white or blue when cold are just some of the signs you could have Lupus. Lupus has been called "the great imitator" because its symptoms are similar to those of many other diseases and conditions including rheumatoid arthritis, a blood disorder, fibromyalgia, diabetes, a thyroid issue, Lyme disease, or any number of heart, lung, muscle, and bone diseases.

Lupus is a disease in which the immune system isn't working right. A healthy immune system fights off invaders and prevents them from hurting you, like viruses (the flu), bacteria, and germs. But someone with Lupus has an immune system that is "autoimmune," which means it can't tell the difference between healthy tissues and invaders—so it actually produces "autoantibodies" to attack the healthy tissues, causing pain, swelling, and damage to the body.

The symptoms of Lupus get worse when someone is under stress or ill. These are called stressors. The extent of the disease can range in severity from person to person—so one person may have a more severe case that needs more treatment than someone else with a less active case. It is not contagious. Most people who develop it are young—between the ages of 15–44.

It is estimated that about 1.5 million Americans have Lupus—including Selena Gomez.

Just after Christmas in 2013 a report was published that an unnamed source close to Selena said the actress and singer had Lupus. In the summer of 2014, her grandfather Ricardo Gomez Sr. gave an interview to Radar Online and confirmed that a few years ago his granddaughter was diagnosed with Lupus.

with Lupus, an autoimmune disease that results in the body attacking healthy tissue. Hispanics are more commonly afflicted with the disease and 90 percent of all those who have the condition are women.

Woman of the Year

In 2012, Selena Gomez was named as *Glamour* magazine's Woman of the Year. The award was bestowed upon the young star not just because of her successful career as an actress and musician but also because of her passion for helping others.

"She's giving back to people who need help, because of her own life experience," said Taylor Swift. "She's the exception to so many rules."[7]

The title meant everything to Selena because the work she does to help others is extremely important to her and more publicity means more money raised for the causes she supports. "I'm going to hold it close to my heart," Selena said.[8]

Chapter 10

OVER THE RAINBOW

Childhood favorite *The Wizard of Oz* remains one of Selena Gomez's favorite movies. The song "Somewhere Over the Rainbow" resonates with her today just as strongly as it did when she first sang it playing Gianna on *Barney & Friends*. "My mom read that book to me and then I read it over and over," Selena said. "I loved Dorothy and I loved the characters and I have the movie. I have no idea why, but I just loved that book."[1]

Changes

There have been a lot of changes in Selena's life since her seventh birthday when she was one of 1,400 young girls standing in line one hot summer day vying for a spot on the popular children's show. Most recently those changes have included a new home, a new manager, new family members, a new boyfriend, and new career goals.

In May 2014, Selena bought a new home for herself in Los Angeles, a sprawling five-bedroom home with 7,200

Selena Gomez: Pop Singer and Actress

Good friend Taylor Swift wants Selena to move to New York City so the two can spend more time together.

square feet. Her favorite part of home ownership is to finally have the chance to feel like an adult who doesn't have to check in all the time with her mother—even though her mom still checks on her. "My mom is the sweetest ever so even now she checks in on me," Selena said.[2]

Even though she just put down firm roots in California, Selena said her friend Taylor Swift is trying to get her to move to New York. "Yes, she wants to kidnap me," Selena said. "She's been begging me every time I get on the phone with her to move to New York because it's been a really good thing for her. We've been friends for seven years, and she really feels like she stepped into her own and became a woman there. She's like, 'Alright, your turn now come on.' I feel like I might eventually, but not right now."[3]

In spring 2014, Selena made another important move when she made the decision to change her management team from her parents, Mandy and Brian Teefey, who had managed her career since her days at Disney, to Bradford Cobb, who has guided the career of Katy Perry since 2004. Mandy supported the decision and said they still plan to work together on certain projects, including the upcoming film *The Sky is Elsewhere*.

But right now Mandy has other important things to focus on—a new baby girl named Grace who was born June 12, 2013. Selena's father Rick also got married and he and his wife had a baby girl in June 2014—naming

Selena has begun to get parts in more complex movies, such as 2013's *Getaway*, co-starring Ethan Hawke, that show her acting skills.

her Tori. That's two baby sisters now for the once only child.

For now Selena is content with a houseful of dogs named Chip, Willy, Fina, Wallace, Chaz, and Baylor.

The Road Ahead

Shifting from a child star to an adult star is a challenging path fraught with risks. However, it's one she's ready to take, even though she admits to being afraid. "I'm terrified I really am," she says. "I've gained credit in the younger audience within the teen crowd. They've given me a platform that I'm very grateful for and so I never ever want to do anything to push them away or to disappoint them. But now I kind of want be an adult. I kind of want to be taken seriously, and I'd like to work and be seen in a different light."[4]

In the next chapter of her life Selena plans to continue to pursue music, but acting is her top priority. She wants to stay professionally challenged, taking on a variety of roles. "I think in the future Selena is going to make some career choices that shock people in a good way," Taylor Swift said. "She's going to choose movies that are risky and roles that are interesting and just really evoke a lot of emotion."[5]

Selena has already started to take some professional risks appearing in a wide genre of films. In 2012 she took a stark turn from her typical good-girl roles by appearing in *Spring Breakers*, a drama with plenty of drugs, drinking, and crime. She followed that up the next year with the action movie *Getaway* and a smaller

Selena Gomez: Pop Singer and Actress

Even as her acting career soars, Selena loves working on her music. In 2013 she performed at the KISS 108 Jingle Ball.

part in the widely acclaimed drama *Rudderless* about a father dealing with the loss of his son.

In 2015 she began filming *In Dubious Battle*, a drama about an activist involved in the farm workers labor movement in the 1930s. It's directed by her *Spring Breakers* co-star James Franco. She's also starring in *The Revised Fundamentals of Caregiving*, a drama also starring Paul Rudd about a man who had experienced a great deal of loss and enrolls in a class that changes his outlook on life.

Be True to You

Keeping it real is important to Selena. She knows the superficial aspects of the business are unhealthy and easy to get caught up in, so she makes a point of surrounding herself with people who keep her grounded and normal. This includes close friends, family, and—first and foremost—her mother.

Taylor Swift thinks that the most important thing to know about Selena is that she's abnormally talented but at her core she's normal. Her father knows that one of the most important things in her life—is her fans. They mean the world to her. Her cousin Priscilla DeLeon doesn't think Selena has changed much at all over the years. "The Selena I grew up with is still the same Selena I see today," DeLeon said. "The only thing that I believe Selena has changed is the way she dresses…now she's a fashionista."[6]

Being a role model was never something Selena aspired to be—but one day she realized it was her destiny.

"I never really said I want to be a role mode but then when it happened I was so down for it," she said. Once I realized that I had a little girl come up to you and say she wants to be just like you it was beautiful—and I accept it. I'm human I'm not perfect. I make mistakes all the time but I guess my job is to keep those mistakes to myself and just try to be the best I can be for those kids."[7]

Can You Hear the Music?

Unlike her contemporaries, Selena didn't rush into a record deal, choosing to focus instead on acting. And when she finally did sign a music deal at the age of 16, she was determined to be in a band that didn't include her name. But record executives convinced her to use her name and Selena Gomez & the Scene was born. Members include bassist Joey Clement, drummer Greg Garman, keyboardist Dane Forrest, and guitarist Drew Taubenfeld. They recorded three studio albums, one remix album, seven singles, and seven music videos. The second single from the album, *Naturally*, reached the top thirty in the United States, the top twenty in New Zealand, Canada, and Germany and the top ten in both Ireland and the United Kingdom. The song has also been certified platinum in the United States and Canada. Their second album, *A Year Without Rain* was released on September 17, 2010. It debuted on the US Billboard 200 at number four and was certified Gold by the Recording Industry Association of America (RIAA) in January 2011. Two singles were released from the album, "Round & Round" and "A Year Without Rain."

As of March 2012 when the band went on hiatus—they had sold over 5 million albums worldwide.

Gomez released her debut solo album, *Stars Dance*, in 2013, followed in 2014 by a greatest hits album, which concluded her contract with Hollywood Records.

You Look Marvelous

Selena is also a successful entrepreneur, having started a clothing line called Dream Out Loud by Selena Gomez sold exclusively through Kmart. She also launched NEO Spring 2015, a collection of glam sportswear for Adidas.

As for the Boys

Selena is tight-lipped about who she dates and rightly so—her relationship with Justin Bieber was a constant subject of public interest. Today she looks for simple qualities in a partner. "Honesty, of course trust, being faithful, making me laugh, those are all the dream right?," Selena said. "It will happen. I don't want to force anything. Just somebody you can enjoy living life with, that you can make fun of stuff [with], have someone you can take to dinners."[8]

Recently, Selena found someone she enjoys spending time with—Anton Zaslavski, a Russian-German music producer and DJ—who prefers to be called by the name Zedd. "He's this cute little German, and he's got really beautiful eyes, and he's very sweet and funny," Selena said. "I respect his vision because he has a way of knowing how important his role is as an EDM (electronic dance music) artist, and he doesn't spend most of his

Change of Scenery?

While many 16-year-old girls would jump at the chance to sign a recording deal with a major label, it took a lot of negotiation to convince Selena Gomez. At first she said no, wanting to focus on her acting—but eventually after a lot of persuasion from both television and record executives, she agreed. However, she did not want to use her name. She refused to be a solo artist. Selena wanted to be in a band. Influenced by some of her favorite groups like Paramore, she had to be convinced and persuaded again to at least use her name. The label wanted a solo artist but eventually relented—and Selena Gomez and the Scene was signed.

With Selena on vocals, the band also included Ethan Roberts on lead guitar and backing vocals, Greg Garman on drums, Joey Clement on bass guitar, and Nick Foxer on keyboard and backing vocals. Nick Foxer and Ethan Roberts eventually left the band and were replaced by Dane Forrest ad Drew Taubenfeld.

After achieving commercial success and releasing three albums, in late 2012 Selena announced the band was taking a break and would be on hiatus so she could focus on acting—but she insisted they would be back after a while.

In November 2014 Selena signed a solo recording deal with Interscope Records—the same label as Taylor Swift.

time traveling the word DJing. He's great, and he cares so much about the meaning of his songs."[9] They met when a mutual acquaintance thought they should work together. Selena and Zedd decided it was a good idea and they began working on "I Want You to Know."

The couple often is spotted out enjoying dinner dates with friends or traveling together—an official sign that they were are couple came when they were photographed holding hands at a Golden Globes after party. They even have a nickname—Zeddlena.

Over the year's Selena has learned that growing up has its challenges but also many rewards—and she reminds herself often that just being herself is good enough. "I feel like sometimes I am 15 in my heart," she says. "You know, sometimes I just go in waves of being a child and being an adult. It's awkward, I am growing up. I am just trying to figure out who I am," Selena said. "Everyone goes through things, the bad and the good, and at the end of the day, I don't regret anything, it makes me who I am."[10]

Chronology

1992—Born Selena Marie Gomez July 22 in Grand Prairie, Texas to Ricardo Joel Gomez and actress Amanda Dawn (Mandy) Cornett.

1997—Selena's parents separate.

2001-2003—Selena played the role of Gianna on the kid's show *Barney & Friends* alongside her friend Demi Lovato.

2003—Selena lands small role in the movie *Spy Kids 3-D: Game Over*.

2005—She ppears in a small role as Julie on *Walker, Texas Ranger: Trial by Fire*.

2006—She is cast as Emily Grace Garcia in the television show *Brain Zapped*—and recorded a song for the show; the show was not picked up.

2006—Selena lands her first major role as a guest star playing "Gwen" in *The Suite Life of Zack and Cody* on the Disney Channel—as well as a role as the evil Mikayla on *Hannah Montana*.

2007—She lands her first starting role as Alex Russo in the series the *Wizards of Waverly Place*, which premiered October 12.

2008—Selena Gomez and the Scene sign a recording deal with Hollywood Records.

2009—Selena starred in *The Princess Protection Program* with childhood pal Demi Lovato.

2010—Selena and Joey King star in the family movie *Ramona and Beezus*.

CHRONOLOGY

2011—Selena is photographed with Justin Bieber at a *Vanity Fair* Oscar party holding hands—confirming long held speculation they are a couple. She stars in the movie *Monte Carlo*.

2012—The *Wizards of Waverly Place* airs its series finale.

2012—Selena makes a move toward more adult roles by appearing in the movie *Spring Breakers* and *Aftershock*. She also lends her voice to the character of Mavis in the animated film *Hotel Transylvania*.

2013—The cast of *Wizards* reunites for a TV special called *The Wizards Return: Alex vs. Alex*. Selena appears in two movies, including the action move *Getaway*.

2013—Mandy gives birth to a baby girl named Grace.

2014—Selena wins Ultimate Choice Award during the 2014 Teen Choice Awards and Favorite Female Singer at the 2014 Kids Choice Awards. She appears in the movies *Behaving Badly* and *Rudderless*.

2014—Selena announces she is signing with a new manager, Bradford Cobb.

2014—She signs solo recording deal with Interscope records.

2014—Selena's father announces the birth of his daughter, Tori.

2015—Selena begins work on two new dramatic movies: *The Revised Fundamentals of Caregiving* and

In Dubious Battle and once again voices Mavis in *Hotel Transylvania 2*.

2015—Selena and Zedd are photographed holding hands at a 2015 Golden Globes after party.

Chapter Notes

Chapter 1. A Night to Remember

1. Wickman, Kase. "Thank You for Letting Me Do What I Love." August 10, 2014. http://www.mtv.com/news/1894578/selena-gomez-teen-choice-awards-speech-2014/.
2. Ibid.
3. Boardman, Madeline. "Selena Gomez Tears Up, Thanks Fans for Support Amidst Personal Struggles at TCAs." August 11, 2014. http://www.usmagazine.com/celebrity-news/news/selena-gomez-cries-thanks-fans-for-support-amidst-personal-struggles-2014118#ixzz3VDzRdp00.
4. Messer, Leslie. "Why Selena Gomez Checked into Rehab." February 4, 2014. http://abcnews.go.com/Entertainment/selena-gomez-checked-rehab/story?id=22375166.
5. Ornos, Riza. "Kids' Choice Awards 2014: Selena Gomez's Speech, Who Gets Slimed and Other Highlights from the Show." March 31, 2014. http://au.ibtimes.com/kids-choice-awards-2014-selena-gomezs-speech-who-gets-slimed-other-highlights-show-1336439.

Chapter 2. Just a Small Town Girl

1. "E! Online Special: Selena Gomez, Part 1." Posted by Team Selena Gomez. https://www.facebook.com/video.php?v=190246661066485.
2–4. Ibid.
5. Radar Online. "Little Girl Lost? Selena Gomez's Grandparents Reveal How Justin Bieber, Rehab & a

Life-Threatening Illness Have Changed The Girl They Once Knew—PLUS Why She's 'In Treatment.'" May 28, 2014. http://radaronline.com/exclusives/2014/05/selena-gomez-grandparents-reveal-rehab-illness-lupus-justin-bieber/.

6. Ibid.

7. Ibid.

8. "E! Online Special: Selena Gomez, Part 1."

9–12. Ibid.

Chapter 3. Endings and New Beginnings

1. "E! Online Special: Selena Gomez, Part 2." Posted by Team Selena Gomez. https://www.facebook.com/video.php?v=190246661066485.

2–17. Ibid.

Chapter 4. A Natural Talent

1. "From Texas to Hollywood." *People* magazine. July 22, 2009. http://www.people.com/people/archive/article/0.20287090.00.html.

2. Ibid.

3. "E! Online Special: Selena Gomez, Part 2." Posted by Team Selena Gomez. https://www.facebook.com/video.php?v=190246661066485.

4. Ibid.

5. Morreale, Marie. "Star SpotLight: Selena Gomez." Scholastic News Online. September 26, 2008. http://www.scholastic.com/browse/article.jsp?id=3750390.

6. Ibid.

7. "E! Online Special: Selena Gomez, Part 2."

8–17. Ibid.

CHAPTER NOTES

Chapter 5. Leaving Barney Behind

1. Hoff, Richard. "Selena Gomez: I Learned a Lot from Barney." October 9, 2007. http://www.nydailynews.com/entertainment/tv-movies/selena-gomez-learned-lot-barney-article-1.226639.
2. "All About Selena Gomez!" *People* magazine. July 22, 2009. http://www.people.com/people/archive/article/0,,20287091,00.html.
3. "E! Online Special: Selena Gomez, Part 2." Posted by Team Selena Gomez. https://www.facebook.com/video.php?v=190246661066485.
4–10. Ibid.
11. Hoff, Richard. "Selena Gomez: I Learned a Lot from *Barney*."
12. "E! Online Special: Selena Gomez, Part 2."

Chapter 6. Disney Dreams

1. "E! Online Special: Selena Gomez, Part 2." Posted by Team Selena Gomez. https://www.facebook.com/video.php?v=190246661066485.
2. Ibid.
3. "From Texas to Hollywood." *People* magazine. July 22, 2009. http://www.people.com/people/archive/article/0.20287090.00.html.

Chapter 7. There's a New Wizard in Town

1. "E! Online Special: Selena Gomez, Part 3." Posted by Team Selena Gomez. https://www.facebook.com/video.php?v=190246661066485.
2, Firman, Tehrene, "You Won't Believe Why Selena Gomez and Taylor Swift Became Friends." *J-14*

magazine. November 11, 2013. http://www.j-14.com/posts/you-won-t-believe-why-selena-gomez-and-taylor-swift-became-friends-18145.
3. Mazuri, Kevin. "Selena Gomez: When It Comes to Guy Drama and Girl Crimes, Selena Gomez Has It All Figured Out." October 29, 2009. http://www.seventeen.com/celebrity/a5958/selena-gomez-interview/.

4–6. Ibid.

Chapter 8. And Then There was Justin

1. "The View: Interview with Justin Bieber." November 23, 2011. http://www.tv.com/shows/the-view/november-23-2011-1560970/.
2. "Selena Gomez: Dating Justin Bieber is Hard." *J-14* magazine. March 15, 2011. http://www.j-14.com/posts/selena-gomez-dating-justin-bieber-is-hard-3829.
3. Dawn, Randee. "Junk Food Diet Sent Selena to the Hospital." *Today Show.* June 16, 2011. http://www.today.com/id/43424359/ns/today-today_entertainment/t/junk-food-sent-selena-gomez-hospital/.
4. "Late Night with David Letterman: Selena Gomez Interview." CBS. March 18, 2013.

Chapter 9. More to Life than Fame and Fortune

1. UNICEF. http://www.unicefusa.org/supporters/celebrities/ambassadors/selena-gomez.
2. Ibid.

Chapter Notes

3. "Ryan Seacrest Launches 'The Voice' at CHOP." July 15, 2011. http://abclocal.go.com/story?section=news/health&id=8253104.
4. "Selena to the Rescue!" July 22, 2009. http://www.people.com/people/archive/article/0,,20287092,00.html.
5. Ibid.
6. Garibaldi, Christina. "Selena Gomez Named Glamour Woman of the Year." November 1, 2012. http://www.mtv.com/news/1696561/selena-gomez-glamour-woman-of-the-year/.
7. Lealos, Shawn. "Selena Gomez named Woman of the Year by Glamour Magazine." June 16, 2011. http://www.axs.com/news/selena-gomez-named-woman-of-the-year-by-glamour-magazine-16514.
8. Ibid.

Chapter 10. Over the Rainbow

1. Morreale, Marie. "Star SpotLight: Selena Gomez." Scholastic News Online. September 26, 2008. http://www.scholastic.com/browse/article.jsp?id=3750390.
2. Benozilio, Shira. "Selena Gomez Teases Justin Bieber—'Walks Around Naked' In New Home." October 13, 2014. http://hollywoodlife.com/2014/10/13/selena-gomez-naked-ellen-degeneres-interview-watch/#.
3. Ibid.
4. "E! Online Special: Selena Gomez, Part 4." Posted by Team Selena Gomez. https://www.facebook.com/video.php?v=190246661066485.
5. Ibid.

6. Ibid.
7. Ibid.
8. Ishler, Julianne. "Selena Dreams of Faithful Boyfriend: Dissing Justin Bieber?" March 22, 2015. http://hollywoodlife.com/2015/03/22/selena-gomez-justin-bieber-relationship-diss-radio-disney-interview-listen/#.
9. Ibid.
10. Shira, Dahvi. "Selena Gomez: I Don't Regret Anything That's Happened in My Life." http://www.people.com/people/article/0,,20704950,00.html.

Glossary

accolade—An award, commendation, or expression of praise.

blocking—A term used in film and television that refers to where an actor stands during filming and how they interact with others on the set.

green room—A dedicated room in a studio or theater in which performers can relax before, between, or after performances.

lupus—A chronic inflammatory disease that happens when a person's immune system attacks its own organs and tissues.

montage—A collection of work that can include a variety of media like video clips, articles, achievements, or pictures.

paparazzi—The name given to photographers who take pictures of celebrities and other well-known people in order to sell them for profit.

pilot—A test show taped for the purpose of deciding whether it will perform well with audiences and to determine if it should be picked up as a series.

premiere—The first episode of a television show or the first showing of a movie or other medium.

Quinceañera—A coming-of-age birthday party with religious overtones for 15-year-old girls welcoming them to adulthood; typically celebrated in the Latin culture.

red carpet—A long, narrow red carpet on which a distinguished visitor walks.

sitcom—Short for "situation comedy," this is a genre of comedy that features characters sharing a common environment.

soundstage—A space in a movie or television studio for recording dialogue.

spinoff—A television show or other medium that originated from one already established. It typically carries over at least one character or situation from the original show.

subpoena—An official document requiring the receiver to appear in court.

Tejano—Music influenced by Texas and Mexico.

Further Reading

Books

Azzarelli, Ally. *Selena Gomez: Latino TV and Music Star* (Hot Celebrity Biographies). Berkeley Heights, N.J.: Enslow Publishers, Inc., 2011.

Uschan, Michael V. *Selena Gomez* (People in the News). Farmington Hills, Mich.: Lucent Books, 2015.

Web Sites

selenagomez.com
Visit Selena's official Web site for news; tour dates; information on her music, movies, charity work, and fashion line; photos; videos; and more.

selenagomezzone.com
Check out this fan Web site devoted to Selena Gomez.

Index

A
"A Day Made Better," 97–98
The Amazing O'Malleys, 62, 64–66
Another Cinderella Story, 15, 68
Arianators, 10, 14
Austin, Jake T., 67
awards, honors, 7–10, 12, 14–15, 100

B
Banderas, Antonio, 52
Barney & Friends, 38–40, 42, 44–46, 101
Bieber, Justin, 9, 12, 79–89
BMI Pop Awards, 12
books, 74
Brain Zapped, 51
Braun, Scooter, 81
"Burnin' Up," 70
Bush, George W., 19

C
Camp Rock, 70
career
    acting generally, 14–15, 56, 58, 68–69, 105
    acting lessons, 49–51
    childhood, 22–24, 37–38
    made for TV movies, 15, 56, 68
    singing, 12, 52, 70–73, 82, 89, 108, 110
charitable work
    amphibians, 95–97
    animal welfare, 92–95
    children, 97–100
    Programa Puente, 93
    UNICEF, 91–93
Clooney, George, 52
clothing line, 109
Cobb, Bradford, 103
college, benefits of, 35
Cyrus, Miley, 70

D
DeLeon, Priscilla, 26, 28, 44, 107
The Directioners, 10
Disney Worldwide, 54–57, 60
Droke, Samantha, 60

F
fan army, 14
Fan Army Award, 10, 14
focus groups, 63
For You, 89

G

Getaway, 105
Gomez, Amanda (Cornett)
  divorce, 28–32
  early life, 17–18
  education, 18–21, 34, 35
  as inspiration, 9, 15, 37–38
  as manager, 49, 54, 62, 79, 103
  miscarriage, 86
  production career, 58–62
  remarriage, 59–60
  as single parent, 32–35
  as teenage parent, 21–22, 27–28
Gomez, Ricardo (Rick), 17–22, 27–28, 32, 38, 64, 103
Gomez, Selena
  birth, 18
  bullying, teasing of, 44
  character, 107–108, 111
  childhood, family life, 21–26, 32–35
  children, 103
  first kiss, 58
  health issues, 10, 82–86, 98–100
  home ownership, 101–103
  love life, 9, 12, 70–71, 75, 79–89, 109–111
  management team, 49, 54, 62, 79, 103
  naming of, 19
Grande, Ariana, 7, 14
Green Room, 84

H

Hannah Montana, 58, 70
Hasselbeck, Elisabeth, 82
Horton Hears a Who!, 73
Housebroken (Arwin), 58, 60

I

In Dubious Battle, 107
Island Dog, 95

J

Jonas, Joe, 67, 70, 97
Jonas, Nick, 70
Jonas Brothers, 67, 70
Joyner, David, 39
JT Superfans, 10, 14
July Moon Productions, 60–62

K

Kids Choice Awards, 10, 13
King, Joey, 73–75
KISS army, 14
Kit Kat Bar Shake, 86

L

Lady Gaga, 10, 14

INDEX

Latina *vs.* Hispanic, 55
Lautner, Taylor, 75
Lee, Ang, 74
Leno, Jay, 84
Letterman, David, 87
Life of Pi, 74
Little Monsters, 14
Lizzie McGuire, 54
Lopez, Jennifer, 7, 19
The Lorax, 74
Lovato, Dallas, 43, 64, 67
Lovato, Demi, 7, 40–43, 47, 64, 68, 86
Lovato, Madison, 43, 64
lupus, 98–100

M

Marsh, Gary, 54–57, 60, 62, 63, 68
The Meadows, 10
Monte Carlo, 81–82

N

Nickelodeon Slime, 13

O

O'Donnell, Rosie, 13
One Direction, 10, 14

P

paparazzi, 12, 75, 79, 89
Perry, Katy, 10, 14
pilot episodes, 63
population census, 55

The Princess Protection Program, 15, 60, 68

Q

Quinceañera, 24, 25
Quintanilla-Perez, Selena, 19

R

Ramona and Beezus, 73–76
The Revised Fundamentals of Caregiving, 107
Rodriguez, Robert, 51
Rosie's Theater Kids, 97
Rudderless, 105
Ryan Seacrest Foundation, 97

S

Saldívar, Yolanda, 19
Schlitterbahn Waterpark Resort, 52
screenplays, 74
Seacrest, Ryan, 88
Selena Day, 19
The Selenators, 9, 10, 12, 14
Spring Breakers, 87, 105
Sprouse, Dylan, 58
Spy Kids 3-D: Game Over, 51–52
Stallone, Sylvester, 52
Stand by Me, 74
Stepanek, Brian, 60

Stevie Sanchez, 54–56
Stewart, Kristen, 75
Stone, Jennifer, 68
The Suite Life of Zack & Cody, 57–58, 60, 62
Sullivan, Catherine, 49
Swift, Taylor, 7, 10, 70, 103, 107, 110

T

Taylor, Judy, 54
Teefey, Brian, 59, 62, 103
Texas, 30
"The Heart Wants What It Wants," 89
"The Voice," 97
Timberlake, Justin, 10, 14
Twilight New Moon, 75, 76

U

Ultimate Choice Award, 7–9

V

Vancouver, Canada, 75, 76
Villegas, Jasmine, 60

W

When the Sun Goes Down, 82
Wizards of Waverly Place: The Movie, 73, 95
The Wizards of Waverly Place, 14–15, 60, 66–68, 71–72, 78
Woman of the Year, 100

Y

A Year Without Rain, 108

Z

Zaslavski, Anton, 109–111